CAMP AND TRAIL

LECTOR HOUSE PUBLIC DOMAIN WORKS

CAMP AND TRAIL

STEWART EDWARD WHITE

ISBN: 978-93-5614-588-7

Published: 1911

LECTOR HOUSE LLP
E-MAIL: info@lectorhouse.com

From a painting by Fernand Lungren

The Home of the "Red Gods"

CAMP AND TRAIL

BY

STEWART EDWARD WHITE

Author of "The Blazed Trail," "The Pass," etc.

Frontispiece in color by Fernand Lungren
and many other illustrations
from photographs, etc.

1911

PREFACE

AFTER considerable weighing of the pros and cons I have decided to include the names of firms where certain supplies may be bought. I realize that this sort of free advertisement is eminently unjust to other worthy houses handling the same lines of goods, but the case is one of self-defense. In *The Forest* I rashly offered to send to inquirers the name of the firm making a certain kind of tent. At this writing I have received and answered *over eleven hundred* inquiries. Since the publication of these papers in *The Outing Magazine*, I have received hundreds of requests for information as to where this, that, or the other thing may be had. I have tried to answer them all, but to do so has been a tax on time I would not care to repeat. Therefore I shall try in the following pages to give the reader all the practical information I possess, even though, as stated, I may seem unduly to advertise the certain few business houses with which I have had satisfactory dealings. It is needless to remark that I am interested in none of these firms, and have received no especial favors from them.

CONTENTS

LIST OF ILLUSTRATIONS

CHAPTER I

THE WILDERNESS TRAVELER

The First Qualification

MANY people have asked me what, all things considered, is the most valuable quality a wilderness traveler can possess. Always I have replied unhesitatingly; for no matter how useful or desirable such attributes as patience, courage, strength, endurance, good nature, and ingenuity, may prove to be, undoubtedly a man with them but without the sense of direction, is practically helpless in the wilds.

The Sense of Direction

A sense of direction, therefore, I should name as the prime requisite for him who would become a true woodsman, depending on himself rather than on guides. The faculty is largely developed, of course, by much practice; but it must be inborn. Some men possess it; others do not—just as some men have a mathematical bent while to others figures are always a despair. It is a sort of extra, having nothing to do with criterions of intelligence or mental development, like the repeater movement in a watch. A highly educated or cultured man may lack it; the roughest possess it. Some who have never been in the woods or mountains acquire in the space of a vacation a fair facility at picking a way; and I have met a few who have spent their lives on the prospect trail, and who were still, and always would be, as helpless as the newest city dweller. It is a gift, a talent. If you have its germ, you can become a traveler of the wide and lonely places. If you have it not, you may as well resign yourself to guides.

The Sense of Direction

The sense of direction in its simplest and most elementary phase, of course, leads a man back to camp, or over a half-forgotten trail. The tenderfoot finds his way by little landmarks, and an attempt to remember details. A woodsman adds to this the general "lay" of the country, the direction its streams ought to flow, the course the hills must take, the dip of strata, the growth of trees. So if the tenderfoot forgets whether he turns to right or left at a certain half-remembered burnt stub, he is lost. But if at the same point the woodsman's memory fails him, he turns unhesitatingly to the left, because he knows by all the logic of nature's signboards that the way must be to the left. A good mountaineer follows the half-obliterated trails as much by his knowledge of where a trail *must* go, as by the sparse indications that men have passed that way. I have traveled all day in the Sierras over apparently virgin country. Yet every few hours we would come on the traces of an old trail. We were running in and out of it all day; and at night we camped by it.

That is, as I have said, elementary. It has to do with a country over which your woodsman has already traveled, or about which he knows something. In the last analysis, however, it means something more.

The sense of direction will take a man through a country of which he knows nothing whatever. He travels by the *feel* of it, he will tell you. This means that his experience subconsciously arranges certain factors from which the sixth sense we are discussing draws certain deductions. A mountaineer, for example, recognizes the altitude by the vegetation. Knowing the altitude he knows also the country formation, and so he can tell at once whether the cañon before him will narrow to an impassable gorge, or remain open enough to admit of passage. This in turn determines whether he shall choose the ravines or ridges in crossing a certain divide, and exactly how he can descend on the other side. The example is one of the simpler. A good man thus noses his way through a difficult country with considerable accuracy where a tenderfoot would become speedily lost.

Thoroughness

Be Sure You Are Right

But if a sense of direction is the prime requisite, thoroughness presses it close. It is sometimes very difficult to command the necessary patience. At the end of a hard day, with the almost moral certainty that the objective point is just ahead, it is easy, fatally easy, when the next dim blaze does not immediately appear, to say to oneself—"Oh, it's near enough"—and to plunge ahead. And then, nine times out of ten, you are in trouble. "I guess this is all right" has lost many a man; and the haste too great to be sure—and then again sure—has had many fatal results. If it is a trail, then be certain you see indications before proceeding. Should they fail, then go back to the last indication and start over again. If it is new country, then pick up every consideration in your power, and balance them carefully before making the smallest decision. And all the time keep figuring. Once having decided on a route, do not let the matter there rest. As you proceed keep your eyes and mind busy, weighing each bit of evidence. And if you become suspicious that you are on the wrong tack, turn back unhesitatingly, no matter how time presses.

A recent expedition with a fatal termination illustrates this point completely. At first sight it may seem invidious to call attention to the mistakes of a man who has laid down his life in payment for them. But it seems to me that the chief value of such sad accidents—beyond the lessons of courage, endurance, comradeship, devotion, and beautiful faith—lies in the lesson and warning to those likely to fall into the same blunders. I knew Hubbard, both at college and later, and admire and like him. I am sure he would be the first to warn others from repeating his error.

Fatal Result of not Being Sure

The expedition of which I speak started out with the purpose of exploring

Labrador. As the season is short some haste was necessary. The party proceeded to the head of a certain lake into which they had been told they would find a river flowing. They found a river, ascended it, were conquered by the extreme difficulties of the stream, one of the party perished, and the others came near to it.

As for the facts so far: The first thought to occur to a man entirely accustomed to wilderness travel would be, is there perhaps another stream? another river flowing into that lake? Encountering difficulties he would become more and more uneasy as to that point, until at last he would have detached a scout to make sure.

But mark this further: The party's informants had told Hubbard that he would find the river easily navigable for eighteen miles. As a matter of fact the expedition ran into shallows and rapids *within a half mile of the lake.*

What Should Have Been Done

To a woodsman the answer would have stood out as plain as print. He would have retraced his way, explored farther, found the right river, and continued. But poor Hubbard was in a hurry, and moreover possessed that optimistic temperament that so endeared him to all who knew him. "They must have made a mistake in the distance. I guess this is all right," said he, and pushed on against difficulties that eventually killed him.

To a man accustomed to exploration such a mistake is inconceivable. Labrador is not more dangerous than other wooded northern countries; not so dangerous as the big mountains; much safer than the desert. A wrong turn in any of these wildernesses may mean death. Forty men succumbed to the desert last summer. Do not make that wrong turn. Be sure. Take *nothing* for granted—either that "they made a mistake in the distance," or that "it's probably all right." One of the greatest of American wilderness travelers knew this—as all wilderness travelers must—and phrased it in an epigram that has become classic. "Be sure you are right, and then go ahead," advised Daniel Boone.

Alertness

So you do not get lost—barring accidents—you are safe enough. But to travel well you must add to your minor affairs the same quality, slightly diluted, perhaps, that I have endeavored to describe above. In this application it becomes thoroughness and smartness. A great many people object while camping to keeping things in trim, to getting up in the morning, to moving with expedition and precision. "Oh, what's the use in being so particular!" they grumble, "this is supposed to be a pleasure trip."

Discipline

Outside the fact that a certain amount of discipline brings efficiency, there is no doubt that a slack camp means trouble sooner or later. Where things are not picked up, something important will sooner or later be lost or left behind. Where the beginning of the day's journey hangs fire, sooner or later night will catch you in a very bad place indeed. Where men get in the habit of slouching, physically and mentally, they become in emergencies unable to summon presence of mind, and incapable of swift, effective movements. The *morale* is low; and exclusive of the fact that such things are an annoyance to the spirit, they may in some exceptional occasion give rise to serious trouble. Algernon is ten minutes slow in packing his horse; and Algernon gets well cursed. He is hurt as to the soul, and demands of himself aggrievedly how ten minutes can be valued so high. It is not the ten minutes as a space of time, but as a measure of incompetence. This pack train is ten minutes short of what a pack train should be; and if the leader's mind is properly constructed, he is proportionately annoyed.

Although not strictly germane to a discussion of equipments, I am tempted to hold up a horrible example.

A Horrible Example

One evening we were all sitting around a big after-dinner fire at the Forest Supervisor's summer camp in the mountains, when an outfit drifted in and made camp a few hundred yards down stream. After an interval the leader of the party came over and introduced himself.

A Horrible Example

He proved to be a youngish man, with curly hair, regular features, a good physique, and eyes handsome, but set too close together. A blue flannel shirt whose top button was unfastened, rolled back to show his neck; a handkerchief was knotted below that; in all his external appearance he leaned toward the foppish-picturesque. This was in itself harmless enough. Shortly he began to tell us things. He confided that his chief ambition was to rope a bear; he related adventures in the more southern mountains; he stated that he intended to travel up through the Minarets and over Agnew's Pass, and by way of Tuolumne. This was to consume two weeks! Finally he became more personal. He told us how President Roosevelt when on his Pacific Coast tour had spoken to him personally.

"When the train started," said he, "I ran after it as hard as I could with a lot of others, but I ran a lot faster and got ahead, so the President spoke directly to me—not to the crowd, but to *me!*"

He left us suitably impressed. Next morning his camp was astir at five o'clock—as was proper considering the strenuous programme he had outlined. About seven our friend came over to get his animals, which he had turned out in the Supervisor's pasture over night—ten animals in another man's mountain pasture! We had a shooting match, and talked Reserve matters for just one hour and twenty minutes. Then somebody waked up.

"I wonder what's become of Jones; let's go see."

We went. Jones was standing dusty in the middle of the corral. In his hand he held a short loop not over three feet across. This he whirled forward and *overhand*. Occasionally he would cast it at a horse. Of course the outraged and astounded animal was stricken about the knees, whereupon he circulated the confines of the corral at speed.

On the Trail (from a painting by N. C. Wyeth)

Jones and the Mule

And the animals! At the moment of our arrival Jones was bestowing attention on a dignified and gaunt mule some seventeen hands high. I never saw such a giraffe. Two about the size of jackasses hovered near. One horse's lower lip wabbled abjectly below a Roman nose.

We watched a few moments; then offered mildly to "help." Jones, somewhat heated and cross, accepted. The first horse I roped I noticed was barefoot. So were the others. And the route was over a rough granite and snow country. Thus we formed a procession, each leading some sort of equine freak. It was by now nearly nine o'clock.

Camp we found about half picked up. The other members of the party were nice, well-meaning people, but absolutely inexperienced in the ways of the wilderness. They had innocently intrusted themselves to Jones on the strength of his self-made reputation; and now undoubtedly were taking all this fuss and discomfit quite as part of "roughing it."

Helping the Tenderfeet

When we saw them we were stricken with pity and a kindly feeling which Jones had failed to arouse, so we turned in to help them saddle up.

Jones was occupied with a small mule which he claimed was "bad." He hitched said mule to a tree, then proceeded to elevate one hind leg by means of a rope thrown over a limb. Why he did not simply blindfold the animal no one could tell. We looked forward with some joy to the throwing of the pack-hitches.

A Forest Fire

But at this moment a Ranger dashed up with news of a forest fire over in the Rock Creek country. The Rangers present immediately scattered for their saddle horses, while I took a pack and went in search of supplies.

Shortly after one o'clock I was organized, and departed on the trail of the Rangers. They had struck over the ridge, and down the other side of the mountains. Their tracks were easy to follow, and once atop the divide I could see the flames and smoke of the fire over the next mountain system. Desiring to arrive before dark, I pushed ahead as rapidly as possible. About half way down the mountain I made out dust ahead.

"A messenger coming back for something," thought I.

In ten minutes I was stricken dumb to overtake the Jones party plodding trustingly along in the tracks made by the Rangers.

"Well," I greeted them, "what are you doing over here? A little off your beat, aren't you?"

The members of the party glanced at each other, while Jones turned a dull red.

"Wrong trail, eh?" said he easily; "where does this one go to?"

Jones and the Trail

"Why, this isn't a trail!" I cried. "Can't you see it's just fresh tracks made since morning? This will take you to the fire, and that's about all. Your trail is miles to the north of here."

For the moment he was crushed. It was now too late to think of going back; a short cut was impossible on account of the nature of the country. Finally I gave him a direction which would cut another trail—not where he had intended to go, but at least leading to horse feed. Then I bade him farewell, and rode on to the fire.

We Put Them Right

Long after dark, when hunting for the place the boys had camped, I met that deluded outfit moving supperless, homeless, lost, like ghosts in the glow of the fire line. Jones was cross and snapped at me when I asked him if he wasn't seeing a good deal of country. But I looked at the tired faces of the other members of the party, and my heart relented, and I headed them for a meadow.

"How far beyond is Squaw Dome?" asked Jones as he started.

"Sixteen miles—about," said I.

"About eight hours the way you and I travel, then," said he.

"About eight weeks the way you travel," amended a Ranger standing near.

Two days later a shakemaker came to help us fight fire.

"Oh, yes, they passed my place," said he. "I went out and tried to tell him he was off'n the trail, but he waved me aside. 'We have our maps,' says he, very lofty."

Twelve days subsequently I rode a day and a half to Jackass Meadow. They told us the Jones party just passed! I wonder what became of them, and how soon their barefooted horses got tender.

Now the tenderfoot one helps out, nor makes fun of, for he is merely inexperienced and will learn. But this man is in the mountains every summer. He likewise wishes to rope bears.

An Object Lesson

No better example could be instanced as to the value of camp alertness, efficiency, the use of one's head, and the willingness to take advice. I had with me at the time a younger brother whom I was putting through his first paces; and Jones was to me invaluable as an object lesson.

The purpose of this chapter is not to tell you how to do things, but how to go at them. If you can keep from getting lost, and if you can *keep awake,* you will at least reach home safe. Other items of mental and moral equipment you may need will come to you by natural development in the environment to which the wild life brings you.

CHAPTER II
COMMON SENSE IN THE WILDERNESS

Overburdening

THERE is more danger that a man take too much than too little into the wilderness. No matter how good his intentions may be, how conscientiously he may follow advice, or how carefully he may examine and re-examine his equipment, he will surely find that he is carrying a great many pounds more than his companions, the professionals at the business. At first this may affect him but little. He argues that he is constructed on a different pattern from these men, that his training and education are such as to have developed in him needs and habits such as they have never known. Preconceived notions, especially when one is fairly brought up in their influence, are most difficult to shake off. Since we have worn coats all our lives, we include a coat in our list of personal apparel just as unquestionably—even as unthinkingly—as we should include in our calculations air to breathe and water to drink. The coat is an institution so absolutely one of man's invariable garments that it never even occurs to him to examine into its use or uselessness. In like manner no city dweller brought up in proximity to laundries and on the firm belief that washing should be done all at once and at stated intervals can be convinced that he can keep clean and happy with but one shirt; or that more than one handkerchief is a superfluity.

Elimination

Yet in time, if he is a woodsman, and really thinks about such affairs instead of taking them for granted, he will inevitably gravitate toward the correct view of these things. Some day he will wake up to the fact that he never wears a coat when working or traveling; that about camp his sweater is more comfortable; and that in sober fact he uses that rather bulky garment as little as any article in his outfit. So he leaves it home, and is by so much disencumbered. In a similar manner he will realize that with the aid of cold-water soap the shirt he wears may be washed in one half hour and dried in the next. Meanwhile he dons his sweater, A handkerchief is laundered complete in a quarter of an hour. Why carry extras, then, merely from a recollection of full bureau drawers?

Essentials

In this matter it is exceedingly difficult to be honest with oneself. The best test is that of experience. What I have found to be of no use to me, may measure the difference between comfort and unhappiness to another man. Carry only essentials: but the definition of the word is not so easy. *An essential is that which, by each man's individual experience, he has found he cannot do without.*

How to Determine Essentials

How to determine that? I have elsewhere indicated[1] a practical expedient, which will however, bear repetition here. When you have reached home after your trip, turn your duffle bag upside down on the floor. Separate the contents into three piles. Let pile No. 1 include those articles you have used every day—or nearly that often; let pile No. 2 comprise those you have used but once; and pile No. 3 those you have not used at all. Now, no matter how your heart may yearn over the Patent Dingbat in No. 3, shut your eyes and resolutely discard the two latter piles.

Naturally, if you are strong-minded, pile No. 1 will be a synonym for your equipment. As a matter of fact you will probably not be as strong-minded as that. You will argue to yourself somewhat in this fashion:

"Yes, that is all very well; but it was only a matter of sheer chance that the Patent Dingbat is not in pile No. 1. To be sure, I did not use it on this particular trip; but in other conditions I might need it every day."

The Philosophy of Duffle

So you take it, and keep on taking it, and once in a great while you use it. Then some day you wake up to two more bits of camp philosophy which you formulate to yourself about as follows: *An article must pay in convenience or comfort for the trouble of its transportation;* and *Substitution, even imperfect, is better than the carrying of special conveniences*. Then he hurls said Patent Dingbat into the nearest pool.

Patent Dingbats

That hits directly at the weak point of the sporting catalogues. Every once in a while an enthusiast writes me of some new and handy kink he is ready to swear by. It is indeed handy; and if one could pluck it from the nearest bush when occasion for its use arose, it would be a joy and a delight. But carrying it four hundred miles to that occasion for its use is a very different matter. The sporting catalogues are full of very handy kinks. They are good to fool with and think about, and plan over in the off season; but when you pack your duffle bag you'd better put them on a shelf.

Occasionally, but mighty seldom, you will find that something you need very much has gone into pile No. 3. Make a note of it. But do not be too hasty to write it down as part of your permanent equipment.

You Must Not Mind Getting Wet Sometimes

The first summer I spent in the Sierras I discovered that small noon showers needed neither tent nor slicker. So next year I left them home, and was, off and on, plenty wet and cold. Immediately I jumped to the conclusion that I had made a

[1] The Forest.

mistake. It has not rained since. So I decided that sporadic heavy rains do not justify the transportation of two cumbersome articles. Now when it rains in daytime I don't mind getting a little wet—for it is soon over; and at night an adequate shelter can be built of the tarpaulin and a saddle blanket. In other words the waterproofs could not pay, in the course of say three-days' rain in a summer, for the trouble of their transportation during four months.

As I have said, the average man, with the best intentions, will not go too light, and so I have laid especial emphasis on the necessity of discarding the unessential. But there exists a smaller class who rush to the opposite extreme.

Another Sort of Tenderfoot

We all know the type. He professes an inordinate scorn for comfort of all sorts. If you are out with him you soon discover that he has a vast pride in being able to sleep on cobblestones—and does so at the edge of yellow pines with their long needles. He eats badly cooked food. He stands—or perhaps I should say poses—indifferent to a downpour when every one else has sought shelter. In a cold climate he brings a single thin blanket. His slogan seems to be: "This is good enough for me!" with the unspoken conclusion, "if it isn't good enough for you fellows, you're pretty soft."

The Tough Youth

The queer part of it is he usually manages to bully sensible men into his point of view. They accept his bleak camps and voluntary hardships because they are ashamed to be less tough than he is. And in town they are abashed before him when with a superior, good-natured, and tolerant laugh he tells the company in glee of how you brought with you a little pillow-case to stuff with moss. "Bootleg is good enough for me!" he cries; and every one marvels at his woodsmanship.

As a plain matter of fact this man is the worse of two types of tenderfoot. The greenhorn does not know better; but this man should. He has mistaken utterly the problem of the wilderness. The wild life is not to test how much the human frame can endure—although that often enough happens—but to test how well the human wits, backed by an enduring body, can answer the question of comfort. Comfort means minimum equipment; comfort means bodily ease. The task is to balance, to reconcile these apparently opposing ideas.

The Logic of Woodcraft

A man is skillful at woodcraft just in proportion as he approaches this balance. Knowing the wilderness he can be comfortable when a less experienced man would endure hardships. Conversely, if a man endures hardships where a woodsman could be comfortable, it argues not his toughness, but his ignorance or foolishness, which is exactly the case with our blatant friend of the drawing-room reputation.

The author doing a little washing on his own account

Probably no men endure more hardships than do those whose professions call them out of doors. But they are unavoidable hardships. The cowboy travels with a tin cup and a slicker; the cruiser with a twenty-pound pack; the prospector with a half blanket and a sack of pilot bread—when he has to. But on round-up, when the chuck wagon goes along, the cow-puncher has his "roll"; on drive with the wangan the cruiser sends his ample "turkey"; and the prospector with a burro train takes plenty to keep him comfortable. Surely even the Tough Youth could hardly accuse these men of being "soft."

Outfit Should Correspond to Means of Transportation

You must in this matter consider what your means of transportation are to be. It would be as foolish to confine your outfit for pack horses to the equipment you would carry on your own back in the forests, as it would be to limit yourself to a pack horse outfit when traveling across country in a Pullman car. When you have horses it is good to carry a few—a very few—canned goods. The corners of the kyacks will accommodate them; and once in a blue moon a single item of luxury chirks you up wonderfully and gives you quite a new outlook on life. So you chuck them in, and are no more bothered by them until the psychological moment.

On a walking trip, however, the affair is different. You can take canned goods, if you want to. But their transportation would require another Indian; another Indian means more grub and more equipment; and so at the last you find yourself at the head of an unwieldy caravan. You find it much pleasanter to cut the canned goods, and to strike out with a single companion.

Common Sense Should Rule

After all, it is an affair of common sense; but even common sense when confronted by a new problem, needs a certain directing. The province of these articles is to offer that direction; I do not claim that my way is the only way, nor am I rash enough to claim it is the best way. But it is my way, and if any one will follow it, he will be as comfortable and as well suited as I am, which is at least better than going it blind.

CHAPTER III

PERSONAL EQUIPMENT

IN discussion of the details of equipment, I shall first of all take up in turn each and every item you could possibly need, whether you intend to travel by horse, by canoe, or on your own two feet. Of course you will not carry all of these things on any one trip. What is permissible for horse traveling would be absurd for a walking trip; and some things—such as a waterproof duffle bag—which you would need on a foot tramp, would be useless where you have kyacks and a tarpaulin to protect your belongings. Therefore I shall first enumerate all articles of all three classes of equipment; and then in a final summary segregate them into their proper categories.

Concerning Hats

Stetson Hat the Best

Long experience by men practically concerned seems to prove that a rather heavy felt hat is the best for all around use. Even in hot sun it seems to be the most satisfactory, as, with proper ventilation, it turns the sun's rays better even than light straw. Witness the Arizona cowboy on his desert ranges. You will want a good hat, the best in material that money can buy. A cheap article sags in the brim, tears in the crown, and wets through like blotting paper the first time it rains. I have found the Stetson, of the five to seven dollar grade, the most satisfactory. If it is intended for woods travel where you are likely to encounter much brush, get it of medium brim. In those circumstances I find it handy to buy a size smaller than usual, and then to rip out the sweat band. The friction of the felt directly against the forehead and the hair will hold it on in spite of pretty sharp tugs by thorns and wind. In the mountains or on the plains, you can indulge in a wider and stiffer brim. Two buckskin thongs sewn on either side and to tie under the "back hair" will hold it on, even against a head wind. A test will show you how this can be. A leather band and buckle—or miniature cinch and latigos—gives added security. I generally cut ample holes for ventilation. In case of too many mosquitoes I stuff my handkerchief in the crown.

Kerchiefs

About your neck you will want to wear a silk kerchief. This is to keep out dust, and to prevent your neck from becoming reddened and chapped. It, too, should be of the best quality. The poorer grades go to pieces soon, and their colors are not fast. Get it big enough. At night you will make a cap of it to sleep in; and if ever you happen to be caught without extra clothes where it is very cold, you will find that the kerchief tied around your middle, and next the skin, will help surprisingly.

Coats

A coat is useless absolutely. A sweater is better as far as warmth goes; a waistcoat beats it for pockets. You will not wear it during the day; it wads up too much to be of much use at night. Even your trousers rolled up make a better temporary pillow. Leave it home; and you will neither regret it nor miss it.

Sweaters

For warmth, as I have said, you will have your sweater. In this case, too, I would impress the desirability of purchasing the best you can buy. And let it be a heavy one, of gray or a neutral brown.

Buckskin Shirts

But to my mind the best extra garment is a good ample buckskin shirt. It is less bulky than the sweater, of less weight, and much warmer, especially in a wind, while for getting through brush noiselessly it cannot be improved upon. I do not know where you can buy one; but in any case get it ample in length and breadth, and without the fringe. The latter used to possess some significance beside ornamentation, for in case of need the wilderness hunter could cut from it thongs and strings as he needed them. Nowadays a man in a fringed buckskin shirt is generally a fake built to deceive tourists. On the other hand a plain woodsmanlike garment, worn loose and belted at the waist, looks always at once comfortable and appropriate. Be sure that the skins of which it is made are smoke tanned. The smoke tanned article will dry soft, while the ordinary skin is hardening to almost the consistency of rawhide. Good buckskins are difficult to get hold of—and it will take five to make you a good shirt—but for this use they last practically forever.

Overshirts

Of course such a garment is distinctly an extra or outside garment. You would find it too warm for ordinary wear. The outer shirt of your daily habit is best made of rather a light weight of gray flannel. Most new campers indulge in a very thick navy blue shirt, mainly, I believe, because it contrasts picturesquely with a bandana around the neck. Such a shirt almost always crocks, is sure to fade, shows dirt, and is altogether too hot. A lighter weight furnishes all the protection you need to your underclothes and turns sun quite as well. Gray is a neutral color, and seems less often than any other to shame you to the wash soap. A great many wear an ordinary cotton work shirt, relying for warmth on the underclothes. There is no great objection to this, except that flannel is better should you get rained on.

Underclothes

The true point of comfort is, however, your underwear. It should be of wool. I know that a great deal has been printed against it, and a great many hygienic principles are invoked to prove that linen, cotton, or silk are better. But experience with all of them merely leads back to the starting point. If one were certain never to sweat freely, and never to get wet, the theories might hold. But once let linen or cotton or silk undergarments get thoroughly moistened, the first chilly little wind is your undoing. You will shiver and shake before the hottest fire, and nothing short of a complete change and a rub-down will do you any good.

Now, of course in the wilderness you expect to undergo extremes of temperature, and occasionally to pass unprotected through a rainstorm or a stream. Then you will discover that wool dries quickly; that even when damp it soon warms comfortably to the body. I have waded all day in early spring freshet water with no positive discomfort except for the cold ring around my legs which marked the surface of the water.

Wear Woolen Underclothes Always

And if you are wise, you will wear full long-sleeved woolen undershirts even on a summer trip. If it is a real trip, you are going to sweat anyway, no matter how you strip down to the work. And sooner or later the sun will dip behind a cloud or a hill; or a cool breezelet will wander to you resting on the slope; or the inevitable chill of evening will come out from the thickets to greet you—and you will be very glad of your woolen underwear.

A great many people go to the opposite extreme. They seem to think that because they are to live in the open air, they will probably freeze. As a consequence of this delusion, they purchase underclothes an inch thick. This is foolishness, not only because such a weight is unnecessary and unhealthful, but also—even if it were merely a question of warmth—because one suit of thick garments is not nearly so warm as two suits of thin. Whenever the weather turns very cold on you, just put on the extra undershirt over the one you are wearing, and you will be surprised to discover how much warmth two gauze tissues—with the minute air space between them—can give. Therefore, though you must not fail to get full length woolen underclothes, you need not buy them of great weight. The thinnest Jaeger is about right.

The Laundry Problem

Two undershirts and three pairs of drawers are all you ever will need on the most elaborate trip. You perhaps cannot believe that until you have gotten away from the idea that laundry must be done all at once. In the woods it is much handier to do it a little at a time. Soap your outershirt at night; rinse it in the morning; dry it on top of your pack during the first two hours. In the meantime wear your sweater; or, if it is warm enough, appear in your undershirt. When you change your underclothes—which should be one garment at a time—do the same thing. Thus always you will be possessed of a clean outfit without the necessity of carrying a lot of extras.

Trousers

The matter of trousers is an important one; for unless you are possessed of abundant means of transportation, those you have on will be all you will take. I used to include an extra pair, but got over it. Even when trout fishing I found that by the time I had finished standing around the fire cooking, or yarning, I might have to change the underdrawers, but the trousers themselves had dried well enough. And patches are not too difficult a maneuver.

Moleskin and Khaki

The almost universal wear in the West is the copper-riveted blue canvas overall. They are very good in that they wear well. Otherwise they are stiff and noisy in the brush. Kersey is excellent where much wading is to be done or much rainy weather encountered—in fact it is the favorite "driving" trousers with rivermen—but like all woven woolen materials it "picks out" in bad brush. Corduroy I would not have as a gift. It is very noisy, and each raindrop that hits it spreads at once to the size of a silver dollar. I verily believe an able pair of corduroys can, when feeling good, soak up ten pounds of water. Good moleskin dries well, and until it begins to give out is soft and tough. But it is like the one-hoss shay: when it starts to go, it does the job up completely in a few days. The difficulty is to guess when that moment is due to arrive. Anything but the best quality is worthless. Khaki has lately come into popularity. It wears remarkably well, dries quickly, and is excellent in all but one particular: it shows every spot of dirt. A pair of khakis three days along on the trail look as though they had been out a year. The new green khaki is a little better. Buckskin is all right until you get it wet, then you have—temporarily—enough material to make three pairs and one for the boy.

The best trousers I know of is a combination of the latter two materials. I bought a pair of the ordinary khaki army riding breeches, and had a tailor cover them completely—fore, aft, and sideways—with some good smoke-tanned buckskin I happened to have. It took a skin and a half. These I have worn now for three seasons, in all kinds of country, in all kinds of weather, and they are to-day as good as when I constructed them. In still hunting they are noiseless; horseback they do not chafe; in cold weather they are warm, and the hot sun they turn. The khaki holds the stretch of buckskin when wet—as they have been for a week at a time. Up to date the smoke tan has dried them soft. Altogether they are the most satisfactory garment of this kind I have experimented with.

There remains the equally important subject of footwear.

Socks

Get heavy woolen lumberman's socks, and wear them in and out of season. They are not one whit hotter on the feet than the thinnest you can buy, for the impervious leather of the shoe is really what keeps in the animal heat—the sock has little to do with it. You will find the soft thick wool an excellent cushion for a long tramp; and with proper care to avoid wrinkles, you will never become tender-footed nor chafed. At first it seems ridiculous to draw on such thick and apparently hot socks when the sun peeping over the rim of the desert promises you a scorching day. Nothing but actual experience will convince you; but I am sure that if you will give the matter a fair test, you will come inevitably to my conclusion.

The Ideal Footwear

If a man were limited to a choice between moccasins and shoes, it would be very difficult to decide wisely which he should take. Each has its manifest advantages over the other, and neither can entirely take the place of the other.

The ideal footwear should give security, be easy on the feet, wear well, and give absolute protection. These qualities I have named approximately in the order of their importance.

Security of footing

Security of footing depends on the nature of the ground over which you are traveling. Hobnails only will hold you on a slope covered with pine needles, for instance; both leather and buckskin there become as slippery as glass. In case of smooth rocks, however, your hobnails are positively dangerous, as they slide from under you with all the vicious force and suddenness of unaccustomed skates. Clean leather is much better, and buckskin is the best of all. Often in hunting deer along the ledges of the deep box cañons I, with my moccasins, have walked confidently up slants of smooth rock on which my hobnailed companion was actually forced to his hands and knees. Undoubtedly also a man carrying a pack through mixed forest is surer of his footing and less liable to turned ankles in moccasins than in boots. My experience has been that with the single exception mentioned, I have felt securer in the buckskin.

Ease

As for ease to the feet, that is of course a matter of opinion. Undoubtedly at first the moccasin novice is literally a tenderfoot. But after astonishingly few days of practice a man no longer notices the lack of a sole. I have always worn moccasins more or less in the woods, and now can walk over pebbles or knife-edge stones without the slightest discomfort. In fact the absence of rolling and slipping in that sort of shifting footing turns the scale quite the other way.

Wear

The matter of wear is not so important. It would seem at first glance that the one thin layer of buckskin would wear out before the several thick layers of a shoe's sole. Such is not always the case. A good deal depends on the sort of ground you cover. If you wet moccasins, and then walk down hill with them over granite shale, you can get holes to order. Boots wear rapidly in the same circumstances. On the other hand I have on at this moment a pair of mooseskin moccasins purchased three years ago at a Hudson's Bay Company's post, which have seen two summers' off and on service in the Sierras. Barring extraordinary conditions, I should say that each in its proper use, a pair of boots and a pair of moccasins would last about the same length of time. The moccasin, however, has this advantage: it can be readily patched, and even a half dozen extra pairs take up little room in the pack.

"Mountain on mountain towering high, and a valley in between"

Waterproofing

Absolute protection must remain a tentative term. No footwear I have succeeded in discovering gives absolute protection. Where there is much work to be done in the water, I think boots are the warmest and most comfortable, though no leather is perfectly waterproof. Moccasins then become slimpsy, stretched, and loathsome. So likewise moccasins are not much good in damp snow, though in dry snow they are unexcelled.

In my own practice I wear boots on a horseback trip, and carry moccasins in my pack for general walking. In the woods I pack four pair of moccasins. In a canoe, moccasins of course.

About Boots

Do not make the common mistake of getting tremendously heavy boots. They are clumsy to place, burdensome to carry, and stiff and unpliable to the chafing point. The average amateur woodsman seems to think a pair of elephantine brogans is the proper thing—a sort of badge of identification in the craft. If he adds big hobnails to make tracks with, he is sure of himself. A medium weight boot, of medium height, with medium heavy soles armed only with the small Hungarian hobnail is about the proper thing. Get them eight inches high; supplied with very large eyelets part way, then the heaviest hooks, finishing with two more eyelets at the top. The latter will prevent the belt-lacing you will use as shoestrings from coming unhooked.

You will see many advertisements of waterproof leather boots. No such thing is made. Some with good care will exclude water for a while, if you stay in it but a few minutes at a time, but sooner or later as the fibers become loosened the water will penetrate. In the case of the show window exhibit of the shoe standing in a pan of water, pressure of the foot and ground against the leather is lacking, which of course makes all the difference. This porosity is really desirable. A shoe wholly waterproof would retain and condense the perspiration to such an extent that the feet would be as wet at the end of the day. Such is the case with rubber boots. All you want is a leather that will permit you to splash through a marsh, a pool, or a little stream, and will not seek to emulate blotting paper in its haste to become saturated.

The Most Durable Boots

Of the boots I have tried, and that means a good many, I think the Putman boot and the river driver's boot, made by A. A. Cutter of Eau Claire, Wis., are made of the most durable material. The Putman boot is the more expensive; and in the case of the three pairs I know of personally, the sewing has been defective. The material, however, wears remarkably well, and remains waterproof somewhat longer than any of the others. On the other hand the Cutter shoe is built primarily for rivermen and timber cruisers of the northern forests, and is at once cheap and durable. It has a brace of sole leather about the heel which keeps the latter upright and prevents it running over. It is an easier shoe on the foot than any of the others, but does not remain waterproof quite so long as the Putman. Although, undoubtedly, many other makes are as good, you will not go astray in purchasing one of these two.

Rubber

No shoe is waterproof for even a short time in wet snow. Rubber is then the only solution, usually in the shape of a shoe rubber with canvas tops. Truth to tell, melting snow is generally so very cold that you will be little troubled with interior condensation. Likewise many years' experience in grouse hunting through the thickets and swamps of Michigan drove me finally to light hip rubber boots. The time was always the autumn; the place was always more or less muddy and wet—in spots of course—and there was always the greater or lesser possibility of snow. My native town was a great grouse shooting center, and all hunters, old and young, came to the same conclusion.

But wet snow, such hunting, and of course the duck marsh, seem to me the only excuses for rubber. Trout fishing is more comfortable in woolen than in waders. The latter are clumsy and hot. I have known of two instances of drowning because the victims were weighted down by them. And I should much prefer getting wet from without than from within.

You will have your choice of three kinds of moccasin—the oil-tanned shoe pac, the deerhide, and the moosehide.

Shoe Pacs

The shoe pac is about as waterproof as the average waterproof shoe, and would be the best for all purposes were it not for the fact that its very imperviosity renders it too hot. In addition continuous wear affects the oil in the tanning process to produce rather an evil odor. The shoe pacs are very useful, however, and where I carry but two pairs of moccasins, one is of the oil tan. Shoe pacs can be purchased of any sporting goods dealer.

Moccasins

The deerhide moccasin, in spite of its thinner texture, wears about as well as the moosehide, is less bulky to carry, but stretches more when wet and is not as easy on the feet. I use either sort as I happen to get hold of them. Genuine buckskin or moose is rather scarce. Commercial moccasins with the porcupine quills and "Souvenir of Mackinaw" on them are made by machinery out of sheepskin. They are absolutely useless, and last about long enough to get out of sight of the shop. A great majority of the moccasins sold as sportsman's supplies are likewise very bogus. My own wear I have always purchased of Hudson's Bay posts. Undoubtedly many reliable firms carry them; but I happen to know by personal experience that the Putman Boot Company of Minneapolis have the real thing.

Waistcoats

Proceeding to more outer garments, a waistcoat is a handy affair. In warm weather you leave it open and hardly know you have it on; in cold weather you button it up, and it affords excellent protection. Likewise it possesses the advantage of numerous pockets. These you will have your women folk extend and deepen for you, until your compass, notebook, pipe, matches, and so forth fit nicely in them. As it is to be used as an outside garment, have the back lined. If you have shot enough deer to get around to waistcoats, nothing could be better by way of material than the ever-useful buckskin.

Waterproofs

I am no believer in waterproof garments. Once I owned a pantasote outer coat which I used to assume whenever it rained. Ordinarily when it is warm enough to rain, it is warm enough to cause you to perspire under the exertion of walking in a pantasote coat. This I discovered. Shortly I would get wet, and would be quite unable to decide whether the rain had soaked through from the outside or I had soaked through from the inside. After that I gave the coat away to a man who had not tried it, and was happy. If I must walk in the rain I prefer to put on a sweater—the rough wool of which will turn water for some time and the texture of which allows ventilation. Then the chances are that even if I soak through I do not get a reactionary chill from becoming overheated.

Ponchos

In camp you will know enough to go in when it rains. When you have to sally forth you will thrust your head through the hole in the middle of your rubber blanket. When thus equipped the rubber blanket is known as a poncho, and is most useful because it can be used for two purposes.

Slickers

Horseback in a rainy country is, however, a different matter. There transportation is not on your back, but another's; and sitting a horse is not violent exercise. Some people like a poncho. I have always found its lower edge cold, clumsy, and wet, much inclined to blow about, and apt to soak your knees and the seat of your saddle. The cowboy slicker cannot be improved upon. It is different in build from the ordinary oilskin. Call for a "pommel slicker," and be sure it is apparently about two sizes too large for you. Thus you will cover your legs. Should you be forced to walk, a belt around your waist will always enable you to tuck it up like a comic opera king. It is sure ludicrous to view, but that does not matter.

Chaparejos

Apropos of protecting your legs, there remains still the question of chaparejos or chaps. Unless you are likely to be called on to ride at some speed through thorny brush, or unless you expect to ride very wet indeed, they are a useless affectation. The cowboy needs them because he does a great deal of riding of the two kinds just mentioned. Probably you will not. I have had perhaps a dozen occasions to put them on. If you must have them, get either oil-tanned or hair chaps. Either of these sheds water like a tin roof. The hair chaps will not last long in a thorny country.

Gloves

You will need furthermore a pair of gloves of some sort, not for constant wear, nor merely for warmth, but to protect you in the handling of pack ropes, lead ropes, and cooking utensils. A good buckskin gauntlet is serviceable, as the cuffs keep the cold breezes from playing along your forearm to your shoulder, and exclude the dust. When you can get hold of the army gauntlet, as you sometimes can in the military stores, buy them. Lacking genuine buckskin, the lighter grades of "asbestos" yellow tan are the best. They cost about two dollars. To my notion a better rig is an ordinary pair of short gloves, supplemented by the close-fitting leather cuffs of a cowboy's outfit. The latter hold the wrist snugly, exclude absolutely chill and dirt, and in addition save wear and soiling of the shirt cuff. They do not pick up twigs, leaves, and rubbish funnel wise, as a gauntlet cuff is apt to do.

That, I think, completes your wearing apparel. Let us now take up the contents of your pockets, and your other personal belongings.

SUMMARY

Minimum for comfort	*Maximum*
Felt hat	Felt hat
Silk kerchief	Silk kerchief
Waistcoat	Waistcoat
Buckskin shirt or sweater	Buckskin shirt and sweater
Gray flannel shirt	Gray flannel shirt
2 undershirts and drawers	2 undershirts, 3 drawers (includes one suit you wear)
Trousers—buckskin over khaki	Trousers
3 pairs heavy socks	4 pairs socks
{ 3 pairs moccasins	1 pair boots
or	Moccasins
1 pair boots	Slicker
1 pair moccasins }	Gloves and leather cuffs
Gloves and leather cuffs	

CHAPTER IV

PERSONAL EQUIPMENT (CONTINUED)

Matches

MATCHES, knife, and a compass are the three indispensables. By way of ignition you will take a decided step backward from present-day civilization in that you will pin your faith to the old sulphur "eight-day" matches of your fathers. This for several reasons. In the first place they come in blocks, unseparated, which are easily carried without danger of rubbing one against the other. In the second place, they take up about a third the room the same number of wooden matches would require. In the third place, they are easier to light in a wind, for they do not flash up and out, but persist. And finally, if wet, they can be spread out and dried in the sun, which is the most important of all. So buy you a nickel's worth of sulphur matches.

Match Safes

The main supply you will pack in some sort of waterproof receptacle. I read a story recently in which a man was recognized as a true woodsman because he carried his matches in a bottle. He must have had good luck. The cardinal principle of packing is never to carry any glassware. Ninety and nine days it may pass safely, but the hundredth will smash it as sure as some people's shooting. And then you have jam, or chili powder, or syrup, or whiskey, all over the place—or else no matches. Any good screw top can—or better still, two telescoping tubes—is infinitely better.

The day's supply you will put in your pocket. A portion can go in a small waterproof match safe; but as it is a tremendous nuisance to be opening such a contrivance every time you want a smoke, I should advise you to stick a block in your waistcoat pocket, where you can get at them easily. If you are going a-wading, and pockets are precarious, you will find your hat band handy.

The waterproof pocket safe is numerous on the market. A ten-gauge brass shell will just chamber a twelve-gauge. Put your matches in the twelve-gauge, and telescope the ten over it. Abercrombie & Fitch, of New York, make a screw top safe of rubber, which has the great advantage of floating if dropped, but it is too bulky and the edges are too sharp. The Marble safe, made by the Marble Axe Company, is ingenious and certainly waterproof; but if it gets bent in the slightest degree, it jams, and you can no longer screw it shut. Therefore I consider it useless for this reason. A very convenient and cheap emergency contrivance is the flint and steel pocket cigar lighter to be had at most cigar stores. With it as a reserve you are sure of a fire no matter how wet the catastrophe.

One of the mishaps to be expected

Knives

Your knife should be a medium size two-bladed affair, of the best quality. Do not get it too large and heavy. You can skin and quarter a deer with an ordinary jackknife. Avoid the "kit" knives. They are mighty handy contraptions. I owned one with two blades, a thoroughly practicable can opener, an awl or punch, a combined reamer, nail pull and screwdriver, and a corkscrew. It was a delight for as long as it lasted. The trouble with such knives is that they are too round, so that sooner or later they are absolutely certain to roll out of your pocket and be lost. It makes no difference how your pockets are constructed, nor how careful you are, that result is inevitable. Then you will feel badly—and go back to your old flat two-bladed implement that you simply cannot lose.

Sheath Knives

A butcher knife of good make is one of the best and cheapest of sheath knives. The common mistake among amateur hunters is that of buying too heavy a knife with too thick a blade. Unless you expect to indulge in hand to hand conflicts, or cut brush, such a weapon is excessive. I myself have carried for the last seven years a rather thin and broad blade made by the Marble Axe Company on the butcher knife pattern. This company advertises in its catalogue a knife as used by myself. They are mistaken. The knife I mean is a longer bladed affair, called a "kitchen or camp knife." It is a most excellent piece of steel, holds an edge well, and is useful alike as a camp and hunting knife. The fact that I have killed some thirty-four wild boars with it shows that it is not to be despised as a weapon.

Compasses

Your compass should be large enough for accuracy, with a jewel movement. Such an instrument can be purchased for from one to two dollars. It is sheer extravagance to go in for anything more expensive unless you are a yachtsman or intend to run survey lines.

Concerning Guns

I have hesitated much before deciding to say anything whatever of the sporting outfit. The subject has been so thoroughly discussed by men so much more competent than myself; there are so many theories with which I confess myself not at all conversant, and my own experience has been so limited in the variety of weapons and tackle, that I hardly felt qualified to speak. However, I reflected that this whole series of articles does not pretend to be in any way authoritative, nor does it claim to present the only or the best equipment in any branch of wilderness travel, but only to set forth the results of my own twenty years more or less of pretty steady outdoor life. So likewise it may interest the reader to hear about the contents of my own gunrack, even though he himself would have chosen much more wisely.

My Rifle

My rifle is a .30-.40 box magazine Winchester, with Lyman sights. This I have heard is not a particularly accurate gun. Also it is stated that after a few hundred shots it becomes still more inaccurate because of a residue which only special process can remove from the rifling. This may be. I only know that my own rifle to-day, after ten years' service, will still shoot as closely as I know how to hold it, although it has sixty-four notches on its stock and has probably been fired first and last—at big game, small game, and targets—upward of a thousand times. I use the Lyman aperture sight except in the dusk of evening, when a folding bar sight takes its place. At the time I bought this rifle the .33 and .35 had not been issued, and I thought, and still think, the .30-.30 too light for sure work on any animal larger than a deer. I have never used the .35, but like the .33 very much. The old low-power guns I used to shoot a great deal, but have not for some years.

Pistol a Handy Weapon

The handiest weapon for a woods trip where small game is plentiful is a single-shot pistol. Mine is a Smith & Wesson, blued, six-inch barrel, shooting the .22 caliber long-rifle cartridge. An eight-inch barrel is commonly offered by the sporting dealers, but the six-inch is practically as accurate, and less cumbersome to carry. The ammunition is compact and light. With this little pistol I have killed in plenty ducks, geese, grouse, and squirrels, so that at times I have gone two or three months without the necessity of shooting a larger weapon. Such a pistol takes practice, however, and a certain knack. You must keep at it until you can get four out of five bullets in a three-inch bull's-eye at twenty yards before you can even hope to accomplish much in the field.

Revolver Experiences

My six-shooter is a .45 Colt, New Service model. It is fitted with Lyman revolver sights. Originally it was a self-cocker, but I took out the dog and converted it to single action. The trigger pull on the double action is too heavy for me, and when I came to file it down, I found the double action caused a double jerk disconcerting to steady holding. Now it goes off smoothly and almost at a touch—the only conditions under which I can do much with a revolver. It is a very reliable weapon indeed, balances better than the single-action model, and possesses great smashing power. I have killed three deer in their tracks with it, and much smaller game. This summer, however, I had the opportunity of shooting a good deal with two I like better. One is the Officer's Model Colt, chambered to shoot interchangeably either the .38 Colt long or short, or the .38 Smith & Wesson special. In finish it is a beautiful weapon, its grip fits the hand, its action is smooth, and it is wonderfully accurate. The other is the special target .44 Russian. The automatics I do not care for simply because I never learned to shoot with the heavier trigger pull necessary to their action.

Shot Guns

I have two shotguns. One I have shot twenty-one years. It has killed thousands of game birds, is a hard hitter, throws an excellent pattern, and is as strong and good as the day it was bought. I use it to-day for every sort of shooting except ducks, though often I have had it in the blinds lacking the heavier weapon. It is doubtful if there are in use to-day many guns with longer service, counting not so much the mere years of its performance, as the actual amount of hunting it has done. The time of its construction was before the days of the hammerless. It was made by W. & C. Scott & Sons, is 16 gauge, and cost $125. My other is a heavily choked Parker twelve. It I use for wild fowl, and occasionally at the trap.

The main point with guns, no matter what the kind, is to keep them in good shape. After shooting, clean them, no matter how tired you may be. It is no great labor. In the field a string cleaner will do the business, but at once when you get to permanent camp use a rod and elbow grease. In a damp country, oil them afresh every day; so they will give you good service. The barrels of my 16 are as bright as new. The cleaning rods you can put in your leather fishing-rod case.

Duffle Bags

Now all these things of which we have made mention must be transported. The duffle bag is the usual receptacle for them. It should be of some heavy material, waterproofed, and should not be too large. A good one is of pantasote, with double top to tie. One of these went the length of a rapids, and was fished out without having shipped a drop. On a horseback trip, however, such a contrivance is at once unnecessary and difficult to pack. It is too long and stiff to go easily in the kyacks, and does not agree well with the bedding on top.

This is really no great matter. The heavy kyacks, and the tarpaulin over everything, furnish all needed protection against wet and abrasion. A bag of some thinner and more pliable material is quite as good. Brown denim, unbleached cotton, or even a clean flour sack, are entirely adequate. You will find it handy to have them built with puckering strings. The strings so employed will not get lost, and can be used as a loop to hang the outfit from a branch when in camp.

Toilet Articles

A similar but smaller bag is useful to be reserved entirely as a toilet bag. Tar soap in a square—not round—celluloid case is the most cleansing. A heavy rubber band will hold the square case together.[2] The tooth brush should also have its case. Tooth wash comes in glass, which is taboo; tooth powder is sure sooner or later to leak out. I like best any tooth soap which is sold in handy flat tin boxes, and cannot spill. If you are sensible you will not be tenderfoot enough to go in for the discomfort of a new beard. Razors can be kept from rusting by wrapping them in a square of surgeon's oiled silk. Have your towel of brown crash—never of any white material. The latter is so closely woven that dirt gets into the very fiber of it, and cannot be washed out. Crash, however, is of looser texture, softens quickly, and does not show every speck of dust. If you have the room for it, a rough towel, while not absolutely necessary, is nevertheless a great luxury.

---

[2] Kephart, in his excellent book on *Camping and Woodcraft,* suggests carrying soap in a rubber tobacco pouch. This is a good idea.

Medicines

By way of medicines, stick to the tablet form. A strong compact medicine case is not expensive. It should contain antiseptics, permanganate for snake bites, a laxative, cholera remedy, quinine, and morphine. In addition antiseptic bandages and rubber or surgeon's plaster should be wrapped in oiled silk and included in the duffle outfit.

The fly problem is serious in some sections of the country and at some times of year. A head net is sometimes useful about camp or riding in the open—never when walking in the woods. The ordinary mosquito bar is too fragile. One of bobbinet that fits ingeniously is very effective. This and gloves will hold you immune—but you cannot smoke, nor spit on the bait.

Fly Dopes

The two best fly dopes of the many I have tried are a commercial mixture called "lollacapop," and Nessmuk's formula. The lollacapop comes in tin boxes, and so is handy to carry, but does not wear quite as well as the other. Nessmuk's dope is:

Oil pine tar	3 parts
Castor oil	2 parts
Oil pennyroyal	1 part

Fly Dopes

It is most effective. A dab on each cheek and one behind each ear will repel the fly of average voracity, while a full coating will save you in the worst circumstances. A single dose will last until next wash time. It is best carried in the tiny "one drink" whiskey flasks, holding, I suppose, two or three ounces. One flask full will last you all summer. At first the pine tar smell will bother you, but in a short time you will get to like it. It will call up to your memory the reaches of trout streams, and the tall still aisles of the forests.

SUMMARY

Minimum for comfort	*Maximum*
Matches and safe	Matches and safe
Pocket knife (2 blade)	Pocket knife
Sheath knife	Sheath knife
Compass	Compass
1 bandana	2 bandanas
Sporting outfit	Sporting outfit
Duffle bag	Duffle bag
Soap and case	Soap and case

Crash towel
Tooth brush
Tooth soap
Shaving set in oiled silk
Medicines and bandages
Fly dope (sometimes)

Crash towel
Bath towel
Tooth brush
Tooth soap
Shaving set in oiled silk
Medicines and bandages
Fly dope and head net

CHAPTER V

CAMP OUTFIT

Tents

IN many sections of the country you will need a tent, even when traveling afoot. Formerly a man had to make a choice between canvas, which is heavy but fairly waterproof, and drill, which is light but flimsy. A seven by seven duck tent weighs fully twenty-five pounds when dry, and a great many more when wet. It will shed rain as long as you do not hit against it. A touch on the inside, however, will often start a trickle at the point of contact. Altogether it is unsatisfactory, and one does not wonder than many men prefer to knock together bark shelters.

Tent Material

Nowadays, however, another and better material is to be had. It is the stuff balloons are made of, and is called balloon silk. I believe, for shelter purposes, it undergoes a further waterproofing process, but of this I am not certain. A tent of the size mentioned, instead of weighing twenty-five pounds, pulls the scales down at about eight. Furthermore, it does not absorb moisture, and is no heavier when wet than when dry. One can touch the inside all he wishes without rendering it pervious. The material is tough and enduring.

"A" Tent Pitched as Shelter.

"Bed in the bush with stars to see"

I have one which I have used hard for five years, not only as a tent, but as a canoe lining, a sod cloth, a tarpaulin, and a pack canvas. To-day it is as serviceable as ever, and excepting for inevitable soiling, two small patches represents its entire wear and tear.

"A" Tent Pitched Between Two Trees.

Don't Use a Tent Curtain

Abercrombie & Fitch, who make this tent, will try to persuade you, if you demand protection against mosquitoes, to let them sew on a sod-cloth of bobbinet and a loose long curtain of the same material to cover the entrance. Do not allow it. The rig is all right as long as there are plenty of flies. But suppose you want to use the tent in a flyless land? There still blocks your way that confounded curtain of bobbinet, fitting tightly enough so that you have almost to crawl when you enter, and so arranged that it is impossible to hang it up out of the way. The tent itself is all right, but its fly rigging is all wrong.

Best Tent Protection from Flies

I have found that a second tent built of cheesecloth, and without any opening whatever, is the best scheme. Tapes are sewn along its ridge. These you tie to the ridge pole or rope of the tent—on the inside of course. The cheesecloth structure thus hangs straight down. When not in use it is thrust to one side or the other. If flies get thick, you simply go inside and spread it out. It should be made somewhat larger in the wall than the tent so that you can weight its lower edge with fishing rods, rifles, boots, sticks, or rocks. Nothing can touch you.

"A" Tent Pitched on Treeless Ground.

Shape of Tent

The proper shape for a tent is a matter of some discussion. Undoubtedly the lean-to is the ideal shelter so far as warmth goes. You build your fire in front, the slanting wall reflects the heat down and you sleep warm even in winter weather. In practice, however, the lean-to is not always an undiluted joy. Flies can get in for one thing, and a heavy rainstorm can suck around the corner for another. In these circumstances four walls are highly desirable.

Method of Tightening Rope.

On the other hand a cold snap makes a wall tent into a cold storage vault. Tent stoves are little devils. They are either red hot or stone cold, and even when doing their best, there is always a northwest corner that declines to be thawed out. A man feels the need of a camp fire, properly constructed.

"A" Tent the Best

For three seasons I have come gradually to thinking that an A or wedge tent is about the proper thing. In event of that rainstorm or those flies its advantages are obvious. When a cold snap comes along, you simply pull up the stakes along one side, tie the loops of that wall to the same stakes that hold down the other wall—and there is your lean-to all ready for the fire.

When you get your tent made, have them insert grommets in each peak. Through these you will run a light line. By tying each end of the line to a tree or sapling, staking out the four corners of your tent, and then tightening the line by wedging under it (and outside the tent, of course) a forked pole, your tent is up in a jiffy. Where you cannot find two trees handily placed, poles crossed make good supports front and rear. The line passes over them and to a stake in the ground. These are quick pitches for a brief stop. By such methods an A tent is erected as quickly as a "pyramid," a miner's, or any of the others. In permanent camp, you will cut poles and do a shipshape job.

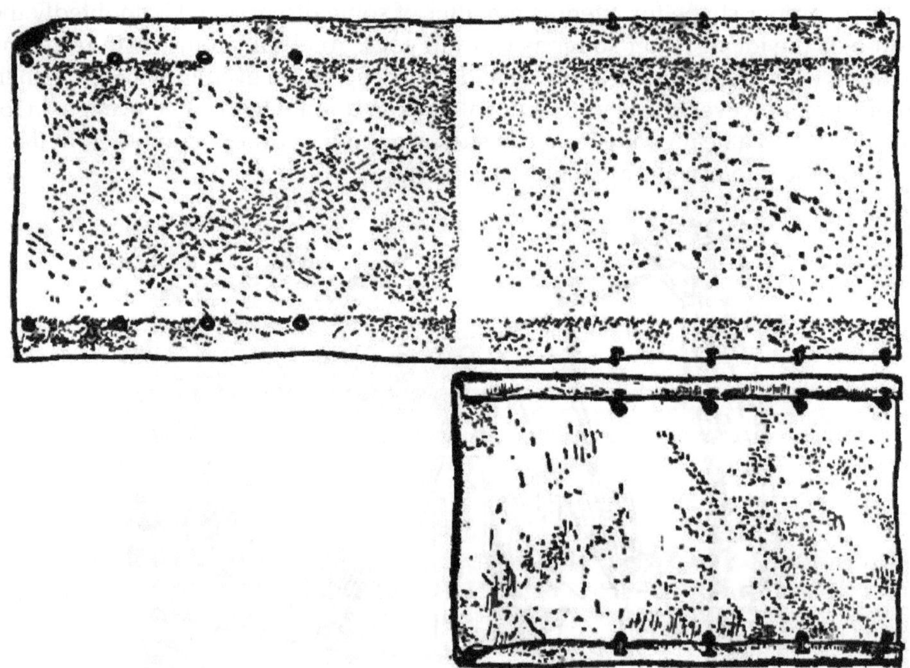

Tarpaulin, Open and Folded.

Tarpaulins

Uses of the Tarpaulin

Often, however, you will not need to burden yourself with even as light a tent as I have described. This is especially true on horseback trips in the mountains. There you will carry a tarpaulin. This is a strip of canvas or pantasote 6 x 16 or 17 feet. During the daytime it is folded and used to protect the top packs from dust, wet, and abrasion. At night you spread it, make your bed on one half of it, and fold the other half over the outside. This arrangement will fend quite a shower. In case of continued or heavy rain, you stretch a pack rope between two trees or crossed poles, and suspend the tarp over it tent wise, tying down the corners by means of lead ropes. Two tarps make a commodious tent. If you happen to be alone, a saddle blanket will supplement the tarp to give some sort of protection to your feet, and, provided it is stretched tightly, will shed quite a downpour.

The tarp, as I have said, should measure 6 x 16. If of canvas, do not get it too heavy, as then it will be stiff and hard to handle. About 10-ounce duck is the proper thing. After you have bought it, lay it out on the floor folded once, as it will be when you have made your bed in it. To the lower half and on both edges, as it lies there, sew a half dozen snap hooks. To the upper canvas, but about six inches in from the edge, sew corresponding rings for the snap hooks. Thus on a cold night you can bundle yourself in without leaving cracks along the edges to admit the chilly air.

Rubber Blankets

In the woods you will want furthermore a rubber blanket. This is unnecessary when the tarpaulin is used. Buy a good poncho. Poor quality sticks badly should it chance to become overheated by the sun.

Blankets

A six or seven pound blanket of the best quality is heavy enough. The gray army blanket, to be purchased sometimes at the military stores, is good, as is also the "three-point" blanket issued by the Hudson's Bay Company. The cost is from $6 to $8. One is enough. You will find that another suit of underwear is as warm as an extra blanket, and much easier to carry. Sleeping bags I do not care for. They cannot be drawn closely to the body, and the resulting air space is difficult to warm up. A blanket you can hug close to you, thus retaining all the animal heat. Beside which a sleeping bag is heavier and more of a bother to keep well aired. If you like the thing occasionally, a few horse blanket pins will make one of your blanket.

To Sleep Warm

It is the purpose of this book to deal with equipments rather than with methods. There are a great many very competent treatises telling you how to build your fire, pitch your tent, and all the rest of it. I have never seen described the woodsmen's method of using a blanket, however. Lie flat on your back. Spread the blanket over you. Now raise your legs rigid from the hip, the blanket of course draping over them. In two swift motions tuck first one edge under your legs from right to left, then the second edge under from left to right, and over the first edge. Lower your legs, wrap up your shoulders, and go to sleep. If you roll over, one edge will unwind but the other will tighten.

Quilts

In the forest your rubber and woolen blankets will comprise your bed. You will soften it with pine needles or balsam. On a horseback trip, however, it is desirable to carry also an ordinary comforter, or quilt, or "sogun." You use it under you. Folded once, so as to afford two thicknesses, it goes far toward softening granite country. By way of a gentle hint, if you will spread your saddle blankets *beneath* your tarp, they will help a lot, and you will get none of the horsey aroma.

Pillows

A pillow can be made out of a little bag of muslin or cotton or denim. In it you stuff an extra shirt, or your sweater, or some such matter. A very small "goose hair" pillow may be thrust between the folds of your blanket when you have a pack horse. It will not be large enough all by itself, but with a sweater or a pair of trousers beneath it will be soft and easy to a tired head. Have its cover of brown denim.

Pails

On a pack trip a pail is a necessity which is not recognized in the forest, where you can dip your cup or kettle direct into the stream. Most packers carry a galvanized affair, which they turn upside down on top of the pack. There it rattles and bangs against every overhead obstruction on the trail, and ends by being battered to leakiness. A bucket made of heavy brown duck, with a wire hoop hemmed in by way of rim, and a light rope for handle carries just as much water, holds it as well, and has the great advantage of collapsing flat.

Wash Basins and Wash Tubs

A wash basin built on the same principle is often a veritable godsend, and a man can even carry a similar contrivance big enough for a washtub without adding appreciably to the bulk or weight of his animal's pack. Crushed flat all three take up in thickness about the space of one layer of blanket, and the weight of the lot is just a pound and a half.

Lanterns

The Stonebridge folding candle lantern is the best I know of. It folds quite flat, has four mica windows, and is easily put together. The measurements, folded, are only 6 x 4 inches by 1-2 inch thick, and its weight but 13 ounces. The manufacturers make the same lantern in aluminum, but I found it too easily bent to stand the rough handling incidental to a horse trip. The steel lantern costs one dollar.[3]

[3] One is now made of brass to fold automatically, at a slightly higher price.

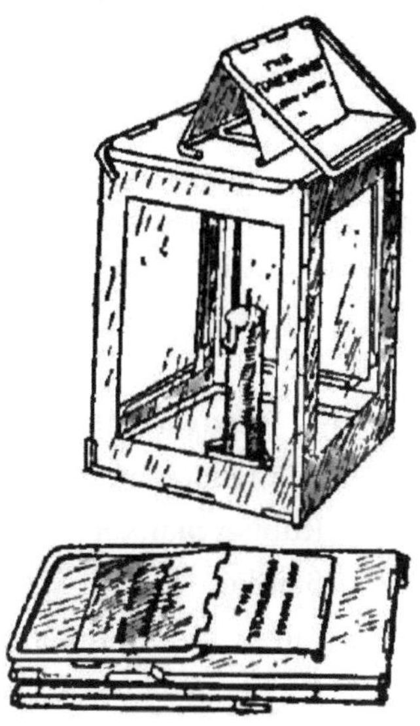

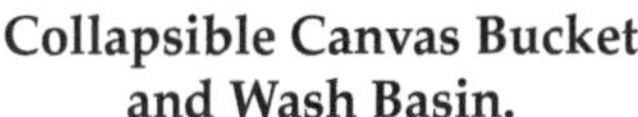

Collapsible Canvas Bucket and Wash Basin.

Folding Lantern.

Hatchets

If you carry an axe at all, do not try to compromise on a light one. I never use such an implement in the woods. A light hatchet is every bit as good for the purpose of firewood, and better when it is a question of tent poles or pegs. Read Nessmuk's *Woodcraft* on this subject. The Marble Safety Axe is the best, both because of the excellent steel used in its manufacture, and because of the ease of its transportation. I generally carry mine in my hip pocket. Get the metal handle and heaviest weight. I have traveled a considerable part of the Canadian forests with no other implement of the sort.

Axes

On a horseback trip in the mountains, however, this will not suffice. Often and often you will be called on to clear trail, to cut timber for trail construction or to make a footing over some ultra-tempestuous streamlet. You might peck away until further orders with your little hatchet without much luck. Then you need an axe—not a "half axe," nor a "three-quarter axe"—but a full five-pound weapon with an edge you could shave with. And you should know how to use it. "Chewing a log in two" is a slow and unsatisfactory business.

To keep this edge you will carry a file and a water whetstone. Use your hatchet as much as possible, take care of how and what you chop, and do not wait until the axe gets really dull before having recourse to your file and stone. It is a long distance to a grindstone. Wes Thompson expressed the situation well. He watched the Kid's efforts for a moment in silence.

"Kid," said he sorrowfully at last, "you'll have to make your choice. Either you do *all the chopping or none of it.*"

Repairs

Needle, thread, a waxed end, and a piece of buckskin for strings and patches completes the ordinary camp outfit. Your repair kit needs additions when applied to mountain trips, but that question will come up under another heading.

SUMMARY

Minimum for comfort	*Maximum*
Silk tent (sometimes)	Tarpaulin
Rubber blanket	Blanket
Blanket	Comforter
Pillow case of denim	Small Pillow
Pocket axe	Canvas bucket
File and whetstone	Canvas wash basin
Needle and thread	Canvas wash tub
Waxed end	Candle lantern and candles
Piece of buckskin	Pocket axe
	5 pound axe
	File and whetstone
	Needle and thread
	Waxed end
	Piece of buckskin

CHAPTER VI

THE COOK OUTFIT

Materials

MOST people take into the woods too many utensils and of too heavy material. The result is a disproportion between the amount of food transported and the means of cooking it.

I have experimented with about every material going, and used all sorts of dishes. Once I traveled ten days, and did all my cooking in a tip cup and on a willow switch—nor did I live badly. An ample outfit, however, judiciously selected, need take up little bulk or weight.

Tin

Tin is the lightest material, but breaks up too easily under rough usage. Still, it is by no means to be despised. With a little care I have made tin coffee pots and tin pails last out a season. When through, I discarded them. And my cups and plates are of tin to this day.

Sheet Iron

Sheet iron had its trial—a brief one. The theory was all right, but in practice I soon found that for a long time whatever is boiled in sheet iron pails takes on a dark purplish-black tinge disagreeable to behold. This modifies, but never entirely disappears, with use. But also sheet iron soon burns out and develops pin holes in the bottom.

Agate Ware

Agate or enamel ware is pleasing to the eye and easily kept clean. But a hard blow means a crack or chip in the enameled surface, and hard blows are frequent. An enamel ware kettle, or even cup or plate, soon opens seams and chasms. Then it may as well be thrown away, for you can never keep it clean.

Iron

A very light iron pot is durable and cooks well. Two of these of a size to nest together, with the coffee pot inside, make not a bad combination for a pack trip. Most people are satisfied with them; but for a perfect and balanced equipment even light-gauge iron is still too heavy.

Aluminum

For a long time I had no use for aluminum. It was too soft, went to pieces, and got out of shape too easily. Then by good fortune I chanced to buy a pail or kettle of an aluminum alloy. That one pail I have used constantly for five years on all sorts of trips. It shows not a single dent or bend, and inside is as bright as a dollar. The ideal material was found.

Short experience taught me, however, that even this aluminum alloy was not best for every item of the culinary outfit.

Utensils

The coffee pot, kettles, and plates may be of the alloy, for it has the property of holding heat, but by that very same token an aluminum cup is an abomination. The coffee or tea cools before you can get your lips next the metal. For the same reason spoons and forks are better of steel; and of course it stands to reason that the cutting edge of a knife must be of that material. The aluminum frying pans I have found unsatisfactory for several reasons. The metal is not porous enough to take grease, as does the steel pan, so that unless watched very closely flapjacks, mush, and the like are too apt to stick and burn. In the second place they get too hot, unless favored with more than their share of attention. In the third place, in the case of the two I have owned, I have been unable to keep the patent handle on for more than three weeks after purchase.

Premising, then, the above considerations, as regards material, let us examine now the kind and variety necessary to the most elaborate trip you will take, at the same time keeping in mind the fact that you can travel with merely a tin cup if you have to.

Made-up Outfits

Do not be led astray into buying a made-up outfit. The two-man set consists of a coffee pot, two kettles, a fry pan, two each of plates, cups, soup bowls, knives, forks, teaspoons, and dessert spoons—everything of aluminum. All fit into the largest kettle, plates and fry pan on top, and weigh but five pounds. The idea is good, but you will be able to modify it to advantage.[4]

A Good Two-Man Outfit

Get for a two-man outfit two tin cups with the handles riveted, not soldered. They will drop into the aluminum coffee pot. Omit the soup bowls. Buy good steel knives and forks with blackwood or horn handles. Let the forks be four-tined, if possible. Omit the teaspoons. Do not make the mistake of tin dessert spoons. Purchase a half dozen of white metal. All these things will go inside the aluminum coffee pot, which will nest in the two aluminum kettles. Over the top you invert four aluminum plates and a small tin milk pan for bread mixing and dish washing. The latter should be of a size to fit accurately over the top of the larger kettle. This combination will tuck away in a canvas case about nine inches in diameter

[4] Abercrombie & Fitch handle the aluminum alloy.

and nine high. You will want a medium-size steel fry pan, with handle of the same piece of metal—not riveted. The latter comes off. The outfit as modified will weigh but a pound more than the other, and is infinitely handier.

There are several methods of cooking bread. The simplest—and the one you will adopt on a foot trip—is to use your frying pan. The bread is mixed, set in the warmth a few moments to stiffen, then the frying pan is propped up in front of the blaze. When one side of the bread is done, you turn it over.

Dutch Ovens

The second method, and that almost universally employed in the West, is by means of the Dutch oven. The latter instrument is in shape like a huge and heavy iron kettle on short legs, and provided with a massive iron cover. A hole is dug, a fire built in the hole, the oven containing its bread set in on the resultant coals, and the hole filled in with hot earth and ashes. It makes very good bread, but is a tremendous nuisance. You have the weight of the machine to transport, the hole to dig, and an extra fire to make. It also necessitates a shovel.

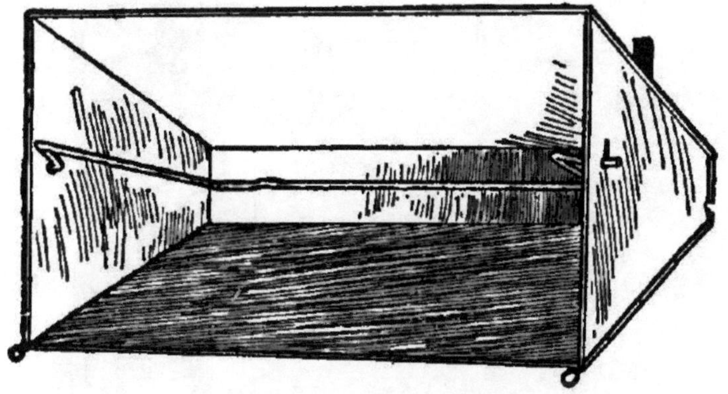

Folding Aluminum Reflector Oven.

Reflector

That the Westerner carries such an unwieldy affair about with him has been mainly, I think, because of his inability to get a good reflector. The perfect baker of this sort should be constructed at such angles of top and bottom that the heat is reflected equally front and back, above and below. This requires some mathematics. The average reflector is built of light tin by the village tinsmith. It throws the heat almost anywhere. The pestered woodsman shifts it, shifts the bread pan, shifts the loaf trying to "get an even scald on the pesky thing." The bread is scorched at two corners and raw at the other two, brown on top, but pasty at the bottom. He burns his hands. If he persists, he finds that a dozen bakings tarnish the tin beyond polish, so that at last the heat hardly reflects at all. He probably ends by shooting it full of holes. And next trip, being unwilling to bake in the frying pan while he has a horse to carry for him, he takes along the same old piece of ordnance—the Dutch oven.

"We may live without friends, we may live without books,
But civilized man cannot live without cooks"

Aluminum Baker

This is no exaggeration. I have been there myself. Until this very year I carried a Dutch oven on my pack trips. Then I made one more try, purchased an aluminum baker of Abercrombie & Fitch, and have had good bread at minimum trouble.

I realize that I seem to be recommending this firm rather extensively, but it cannot be helped. It is not because I know no others, for naturally I have been purchasing sporting goods and supplies in a great many places and for a good many years. Nor do I recommend everything they make. Only along some lines they have carried practical ideas to their logical conclusion. The Abercrombie & Fitch balloon silk tents, food bags, pack harness, aluminum alloys, and reflector ovens completely fill the bill. And as they cannot be procured elsewhere, I must perhaps seem unduly to advertise this one firm.

Their aluminum baker, then, I found to be a joy. I put the bread in the pan, stuck the reflector in front of my regular cooking fire, and went ahead with dinner. It required absolutely no more attention. By the time I was ready to dish up grub, the bread was done. That was all there was to it. The angles are correct, and the aluminum is easily kept bright. When not in use it folds to an inch thick, and about a foot by a foot and a half. It weighs only about two pounds. A heavy canvas case protects it and the bread pan. I pack it between blankets, and never know it is there; whereas the Dutch oven was always a problem. The cost was three dollars.

Food Bags

Food is best transported in bags. Cotton drill, or even empty flour sacks are pretty good on a pack horse; but in canoe and forest traveling you will want something waterproof. Even horseback a waterproof bag is better, for it keeps out the dust. Again I must refer you to Abercrombie & Fitch. Their food bags are of light, waterproof, and durable material, and cost only from a dollar to a dollar and a half a dozen, according to size.

Use of Parallel Logs.

Fire Irons

Of course on a tramp you will carry no extra conveniences in the way of fire irons, but will use as cooking range two green logs laid nearly parallel, or rocks placed side by side. But with a pack horse, there is no reason why you should not relieve yourself of this bother.

Usually two pieces of strap iron about thirty inches long and an inch wide are employed for this purpose. The ends are rested on two stones and the fire built beneath them. In case stones lack, a small trench is dug, and the irons laid across that.

Use of Ordinary Fire Irons.

The Ernest Britten Fire Irons.

The Britten Fire Irons

Inspirator

Mr. Ernest Britten, a Forest Ranger, has however invented a contrivance that is much better. The irons, instead of being made of strap iron, are of angle iron. To the inside of the L and at each end sharpened legs are swung on a rivet. A squared outer corner next the angle iron prevents their spreading, but a rounded inner corner permits their being folded flat. When used, the legs are opened and stuck upright in the ground, the irons being arranged parallel at an appropriate distance from each other. Mark these advantages: The irons can be driven to any height from the ground according as fuel is plenty or scarce. They can be leveled absolutely, a thing difficult to accomplish with stones and strap irons. In case the ground is too hard to admit the insertion of the legs in it, they can be folded back, and the irons used across stones in the manner of the old strap irons. Moreover, and this is important, they weigh no more.

I have had presented me by Mr. Robert Logan of New York, so simple, transportable and efficient a device for kindling fires that I have included it in my regular outfit. It consists of a piece of small rubber tube two feet or so in length, into one end of which is forced a brass cylinder three or four inches long. The extremity of this brass cylinder is then beaten out so that its opening is flattened. Logan calls this instrument an "Inspirator."

How to Use the Inspirator

To encourage a fire you apply the brass nozzle to the struggling blaze, and blow steadily through the rubber tube. The result is an effect midway between a pair of bellows and a Bunsen burner.

Until you have tried it you will have difficulty in realizing how quickly wet wood will ignite when persuaded by the Inspirator. I have used it over five months of camping, and never have failed to blow up a brisk blaze in the foulest conditions of weather and fuel. No more heavy chopping for dry heart-wood, no more ashes in the face empurpled by stooping, no more frantic waving of the hat that scatters ashes. Furthermore, the Inspirator's use is not confined to wet days alone. If ever you particularly desire any individual kettle to boil in a hurry, and that utensil sullenly declines to do so, just direct the Inspirator beneath it, and in a jiffy it is on the bubble. When out of use you wrap the rubber tube around the brass nozzle and tuck it away in your waistcoat pocket.

Towels, Soap, etc.

There remains only the necessity of cleaning up. Get three yards or so of toweling and cut off pieces as you need them. Keep them washed and they will last a long time. Borax soap and a cake of Sapolio help; but you can clean up dishes without soap. Long tough grass bent double makes an excellent swab. For washing clothes I have found nothing to equal either Fels-Naphtha or Frank Siddal's Soap. You soap your garments at night, rinse them in the morning—and the job is done. No hot water, no boiling, little rubbing. And the garments are really clean.

SUMMARY

Minimum for comfort	*Maximum*
1 tin cup with riveted handle	Tin cup
1 aluminum coffee pot	Aluminum coffee pot
1 aluminum pail	2 aluminum pails
1 knife, fork, spoon	Knife, fork, 3 spoons
1 aluminum plate	2 plates
Fry pan	Milk pan
Food bags	2 fry pans to nest
Dish towel	Reflector oven
Fels-Naphtha or Frank Siddal's soap.	Food bags
	Fire irons
	Dish towel
	Borax soap
	Sapolio
	Fels-Naphtha or Frank Siddal's soap.

CHAPTER VII

GRUB

Variety

IN no department of outdoor life does the mistaken notion of "roughing it" work more harm. I have never been able to determine why a man should be content with soggy, heavy, coarse and indigestible food when, with the same amount of trouble, the same utensils, and the same materials he can enjoy variety and palatability. To eat a well-cooked dinner it is not necessary to carry an elaborate commissary. In a later chapter I shall try to show you how to combine the simple and limited ingredients at your command into the greatest number of dishes. At present we will concern ourselves strictly with the kind and quantity of food you will wish to carry with you.

Necessarily bulk and weight are such important considerations that they will at once cut out much you would enjoy. Also condensed and desiccated foods are, in a few cases, toothsome enough to earn inclusion—and many are not. Perishability bars certain other sorts. But when all is said and done there remains an adequate list from which to choose.

Luxuries

However closely you confine yourself to the bare necessities, be sure to include one luxury. This is not so much to eat as for the purpose of moral support. I remember one trip in the Black Hills on which our commissary consisted quite simply of oatmeal, tea, salt, and sugar, and a single can of peaches. Of course there was game. Now if we had found ourselves confined to meat, mush, oatmeal pones, and tea, we should, after a little, have felt ourselves reduced to dull monotony, and after a little more we should have begun to long mightily for the fleshpots of Deadwood. But that can of peaches lurked in the back of our minds. By its presence we were *not* reduced to meat, mush, oatmeal pones, and tea. Occasionally we would discuss gravely the advisability of opening it, but I do not believe any one of us down deep in his heart meant it in sober earnest. What was the mere tickling of the palate compared with the destruction of a symbol.

Take Your Pet Luxury

Somewhat similarly I was once on a trip with an Englishman who, when we outfitted, insisted on marmalade. In vain we pointed out the fact that glass always broke. Finally we compromised on one jar, which we wrapped in the dish towel and packed in the coffee pot. For five weeks that unopened jar of marmalade traveled with us, and the Englishman was content. Then it got broken—as they always do. From that time on our friend uttered his daily growl or lament over the lack of marmalade. And, mind you, he had already gone five weeks without tasting a spoonful!

So include in the list your pet luxury. Tell yourself that you will eat it just at the psychological moment. It is a great comfort. But to our list:

Bacon is the stand-by. Get the very best you can buy, and the leanest. In a walking trip cut off the rind in order to reduce the weight.

Ham is a pleasant variety if you have room for it.

Cereals

Flour.—Personally I like the whole wheat best. It bakes easier than the white, has more taste, and mixes with other things quite as well. It comes in 10-pound sacks, which makes it handy to carry.

Pancake Flour, either buckwheat or not, makes flapjacks, of course, but also bakes into excellent loaves, and is a fine base for camp cake.

Boston Brown Bread Flour is self-rising, on the principle of the flapjack flour. It makes genuine brown bread, toothsome quick biscuits with shortening, and a glorious boiled or steamed pudding. If your outfitter does not know of it, tell him it is made at San José, California.

Cornmeal.—Get the yellow. It makes good Johnny cake, puddings, fried mush, and unleavened corn pone, all of which are palatable, nourishing, and easy to make. If you have a dog with you, it is the easiest ration for between-meat seasons. A quarter cup swells up into an abundant meal for the average-sized canine.

Hominy.—The coarse sort makes a good variety.

Tapioca.—Utterly unsatisfactory over an open fire. Don't take it.

Rice, the Ideal Stand-by

Rice.—I think rice is about the best stand-by of all. In the first place, ten pounds of rice will go farther than ten pounds of any other food; a half cup, which weighs small for its bulk, boils up into a half kettleful, a quantity ample for four people. In the second place, it contains a great percentage of nutriment, and is good stuff to travel on. In the third place, it is of that sort of palatability of which one does not tire. In the fourth place it can be served in a variety of ways: boiled plain; boiled with raisins; boiled with rolled oats; boiled, then fried; made into baked puddings; baked in gems or loaves; mixed with flapjacks. Never omit it from your list.

Buy Only the Best Brands

Baking Powder.—Do not buy an unknown brand at a country store; you will find it bad for your insides after a very short use. Royal and Price's are both good.

When you quit the trail for a day's rest

Tea and Coffee.—Even confirmed coffee drinkers drop away from their allegiance after being out a short time. Tea seems to wear better in the woods. Personally, I never take coffee at all, unless for the benefit of some other member of the party.

Potatoes are generally out of the question, although you can often stick a small sack in your kyacks. They are very grateful when you can carry them. A desiccated article is on the market. Soaked up it takes on somewhat the consistency of rather watery mashed potatoes. It is not bad.

Onions are a luxury; but, like the potatoes, can sometimes be taken, and add largely to flavor.

Saccharine Tablets

Sugar.—My experience is, that one eats a great deal more sweets out of doors than at home. I suppose one uses up more fuel. In any case I have many a time run out of sugar, and only rarely brought any home Saxin, crystallose and saccharine are all excellent to relieve the weight in this respect. They come as tablets, each a little larger than the head of a pin. A tablet represents the sweetening power of a lump of sugar. Dropped in the tea, two of them will sweeten quite as well as two heaping spoonfuls and you could never tell the difference. A man could carry in his waistcoat pocket vials containing the equivalent of twenty-five pounds of sugar. Their advantage in lightening a back load is obvious.

Fats.—Lard is the poorest and least wholesome. Cottolene is better. Olive oil is best. The latter can be carried in a screw-top tin. Less of it need be used than of the others. It gives a delicious flavor to anything fried in it.

Mush.—Rolled oats are good, but do not agree with some people. Cream of Wheat and Germea are more digestible. Personally I prefer to take my cereal in the form of biscuits. It "sticks to the ribs" better. Three-quarters of a cup of cereal will make a full supply of mush for three people, leaving room for mighty little else. On the other hand, a full cup of the same cereal will make six biscuits—two apiece for our three people. In other words, the biscuits allow one to eat a third more cereal in half the bulk.

Fruits

Dried Fruit.—This is another class of food almost to be classed as condensed. It is easily carried, is light, and when cooked swells considerably. Raisins lead the list, as they cook in well with any of the flour stuffs and rice, and are excellent to eat raw as a lunch. Dried figs come next. I do not mean the layer figs, but those dried round like prunes. They can be stewed, eaten raw, or cooked in puddings. Dried apples are good stewed, or soaked and fried in a little sugar. Prunes are available, raw or cooked. Peaches and apricots I do not care for, but they complete the list.

A Good Remedy for a Chill

Salt and Pepper.—A little cayenne in hot water is better than whiskey for a chill.

Cinnamon.—Excellent to sprinkle on apples, rice, and puddings. A flavoring to camp cake. One small box will last a season.

Milk.—Some people like the sticky sweetened Borden milk. I think it very sickish and should much prefer to go without. The different brands of evaporated creams are palatable, but too bulky and heavy for ordinary methods of transportation. A can or so may sometimes be included, however. Abercrombie & Fitch offer a milk powder. They claim that a spoonful in water "produces a sweet wholesome milk." It may be wholesome; it certainly is sweet—but as for being milk! I should like to see the cow that would acknowledge it.

Syrup.—Mighty good on flapjacks and bread, and sometimes to be carried when animals are many. The easiest to get that tastes like anything is the "Log Cabin" maple syrup. It comes in a can of a handy shape.

Altitude's Influence on Cooking

Beans.—Another rich stand-by; rich in sustenance, light in weight, and compressed in bulk. Useless to carry in the mountains, where, as a friend expressed it, "all does not boil that bubbles." Unless you have all day and unlimited firewood they will not cook in a high altitude. Lima beans are easier cooked. A few chilis are nice to add to the pot by way of variety.

Pilot Bread or Hardtack.—If you use it at all—which of course must be in small quantities for emergencies—be sure to get the coarsest. It comes in several grades, and the finer crumble. The coarse, however, breaks no finer than the size of a dollar, and so is edible no matter how badly smashed. With raisins it makes a good lunch.

Butter, like milk, is a luxury I do without on a long trip. The lack is never felt after a day or two. I believe you can get it in air-tight cans.

Macaroni is bulky, but a single package goes a long way, and is both palatable and nutritious. Break it into pieces an inch or so long and stow it in a grub bag.

Canned Goods

That finishes the list of the bulk groceries. Canned goods, in general, are better left at home. You are carrying the weight not only of the vegetable, but also of the juice and the tin. One can of tomatoes merely helps out on one meal, and occupies enough space to accommodate eight meals of rice; or enough weight to balance two dozen meals of the same vegetable. Both the space of the kyacks and the carrying power of your horse are better utilized in other directions. I assume you never will be fool enough to weight your own back with such things.

So much for common sense and theory. As a matter of practice, and if you have enough animals to avoid overloading, you will generally tuck in a can here and there. These are to be used only on great occasions, but grace mightily holidays and very tired times.

Now some canned goods make you feel you are really getting something worth while; and others do not.

Corn is probably the most satisfactory of all. It is good warmed up, made into fritters, baked into a pudding, or mixed with lima beans as succotash.

Good and Bad Canned Goods

Peas on the other hand are no good. Too much water, and too little pea is the main trouble, which combines discouragingly with the fact that a mouthful of peas is not nearly as hearty or satisfying as a mouthful of corn.

Tomatoes are carried extensively, but are very bulky and heavy for what you get out of them.

Canned Fruit is sheer mad luxury. A handful of the dried article would equal a half dozen cans.

Salmon.—A pleasant and compact variation on ordinary fare. It can be eaten cold, as it comes from the can; or can be fried or baked.

Picnic Stuff, such as potted chicken, devilled ham and the rest of it are abominations.

Corned Beef is fair.

To sum up, I think that if I were to go in for canned goods, I should concentrate on corn and salmon, with one or two corned beef on the side.

Desiccated Foods

As I mentioned at the beginning of this chapter modern desiccation of foods has helped the wilderness traveler to some extent. I think I have tried about everything in this line. In the following list I shall mention those I think good, and also those particularly bad. Any not mentioned it may be implied that I do not care for myself, but am willing to admit that you may.

Canned Eggs.—The very best thing of this kind is made by the National Bakers' Egg Co., of Sioux City. It is a coarse yellow granulation and comes in one-pound screw-top tin cans. Each can contains the equivalent of five dozen eggs, and costs, I think, only $1.25. A tablespoon of the powder and two of water equals an egg. With that egg you can make omelets and scrambled eggs, which you could not possibly tell from the new-laid. Two cans, weighing two pounds, will last you all summer; and think of the delight of an occasional egg for breakfast! The German canned eggs—Hoffmeir's is sold in this country—are rather evil tasting, do not beat up light, and generally decline sullenly to cook.

Erbswurst

Soups.—Some of the compressed soups are excellent. The main difficulty is that they are put up in flimsy paper packages, difficult to carry without breaking. Also I have found that when you take but two kettles, you are generally hungry enough to begrudge one of them to anything as thin as even the best soup. However, occasionally a hot cupful is a good thing; and I should always include a few packages. The most filling and nourishing is the German army ration called *Erbswurst*. It comes in a sausage-shaped package, which is an exception to the rule in that it is strongly constructed. You cut off an inch and boil it. The taste is like that of a thick bean soup. It is said to contain all the elements of nutrition.

Knorr's packages make good soup when you get hold of the right sort. We have tried them all, and have decided that they can be divided into two classes—those that taste like soup, and the dishwater brand. The former comprise pea, bean, lentil, rice, and onion; the latter, all others.

Soup Tablets

Maggi's tablets are smaller than Knorr's and rather better packed. The green pea and lentil make really delicious soup.

Bouillon capsules of all sorts I have no use for. They serve to flavor hot water, and that is about all.

Desiccated Vegetables come in tablets about four inches square and a quarter of an inch thick. A quarter of one of these tablets makes a dish for two people. You soak it several hours, then boil it. In general the results are all alike, and equally tasteless and loathsome. The most notable exception is the string beans. They come out quite like the original vegetable, both in appearance and taste. I always take some along. Enough for twenty meals could be carried in the inside pocket of your waistcoat.

Julienne, made by Prevet. A French mixture of carrots and other vegetables cut into strips and dried. When soaked and boiled it swells to its original size. A half cupful makes a meal for two. It ranks with the string beans in being thoroughly palatable. These two preparations are better than canned goods, and are much more easily carried.

Potatoes, saxin, saccharine, and crystallose I have already mentioned.

Quantity

That completes the most elaborate grub list I should care to recommend. As to a quantitative list, that is a matter of considerably more elasticity. I have kept track of the exact quantity of food consumed on a great many trips, and have come to the conclusion that anything but the most tentative statements must spring from lack of experience. A man paddling a canoe, or carrying a pack all day, will eat a great deal more than would the same man sitting a horse. A trip in the clear, bracing air of the mountains arouses keener appetites than a desert journey near the borders of Mexico, and a list of supplies ample for the one would be woefully insufficient for the other. The variation is really astonishing.

Therefore the following figures must be experimented with rather cautiously. They represent an average of many of my own trips.

Grub List

ONE MONTH'S SUPPLIES FOR ONE MAN ON A FOREST TRIP

15 lbs. flour (includes flour, pancake flour, cornmeal in proportion to suit)

15 lbs. meat (bacon or boned ham)

8 lbs. rice

½ lb. baking powder

1 lb. tea

2 lbs. sugar

150 saccharine tablets

8 lbs. cereal

1 lb. raisins

Salt and pepper

5 lbs. beans

3 lbs. or ½ doz. Erbswurst

2 lbs. or ½ doz. dried vegetables

2 lbs. dried potatoes

1 can Bakers' eggs.

ONE MONTH'S SUPPLIES FOR ONE MAN ON PACK HORSE TRIP

15 lbs. flour supplies (flour, flapjack flour, cornmeal)

15 lbs. ham and bacon

2 lbs. hominy

4 lbs. rice

½ lb. baking powder

1 lb. coffee

½ lb. tea

20 lbs. potatoes

A few onions

2 lbs. sugar

150 saccharine tablets

3 lb. pail cottolene, or can olive oil

3 lbs. cream of wheat

5 lbs. mixed dried fruit

Salt, pepper, cinnamon

3 cans evaporated cream

½ gal. syrup or honey

5 lbs. beans

Chilis

Pilot bread (in flour sack)

6 cans corn

6 cans salmon

2 cans corned beef

1 can Bakers' eggs

½ doz. Maggi's soups

½ doz. dried vegetables—beans and Julienne.

Don't Figure Grub List too Closely

These lists are not supposed to be "eaten down to the bone." A man cannot figure that closely. If you buy just what is included in them you will be well fed, but will probably have a little left at the end of the month. If you did not, you would probably begin to worry about the twenty-fifth day. And this does not pay. Of course if you get game and fish, you can stay out over the month.

CHAPTER VIII

CAMP COOKERY

Secret of Camp Cookery

THE secret of successful camp cookery is experimentation and boldness. If you have not an ingredient, substitute the nearest thing to it; or something in the same general class of foods. After you get the logic of what constitutes a pudding, or bread, or cake, or anything else, cut loose from cook-books and invent with what is contained in your grub bags. Do not be content until, by shifting trials, you get your proportions just right for the best results. Even though a dish is quite edible, if the possibility of improving it exists, do not be satisfied with repeating it.

This chapter will not attempt to be a camp cook-book. Plenty of the latter can be bought. It will try to explain dishes not found in camp cook-books, but perhaps better adapted to the free and easy culinary conditions that obtain over an open fire and in the open air.

After *bacon* gets a little old, parboil the slices before frying them.

How to Make Bread

Bread.—The secret of frying-pan bread is a medium stiff batter in the proportion of one cup of flour, one teaspoon of salt, one tablespoon of sugar, and a heaping teaspoon of baking powder. This is poured into the well-greased and hot pan, and set flat near the fire. In a very few moments it will rise and stiffen. Prop the pan nearly perpendicular before the blaze. When done on one side, turn over. A clean sliver or a fork stuck through the center of the loaf will tell you when it is done: if the sliver comes out clean, without dough sticking to it, the baking is finished.

In an oven the batter must be somewhat thinner. Stiff batter makes close-grained heavy bread; thin batter makes light and crisp bread. The problem is to strike the happy medium, for if too stiff the loaf is soggy, and if too thin it sticks to the pan. Dough should be wet only at the last moment, after the pan is ready, and should be lightly stirred, never kneaded or beaten.

Biscuits are made in the same way, with the addition of a dessert-spoonful of cottolene, or a half spoonful of olive oil.

Cornbread is a mixture of half cornmeal and half flour, with salt, baking powder, and shortening.

Unleavened Bread

Unleavened bread properly made is better as a steady diet than any of the baking powder products. The amateur cook is usually disgusted with it because it turns out either soggy or leathery. The right method, however, results in crisp, cracker-like bread, both satisfying and nourishing. It is made as follows:

Take three-quarters of a cup of either cornmeal, oatmeal, Cream of Wheat, or Germea, and mix it thoroughly with an equal quantity of flour. Add a teaspoonful of salt, a tablespoonful of sugar, and a teaspoonful of olive oil or shortening. Be sure not to exceed the amount of the latter ingredient. Mix in just enough water to wet thoroughly, and beat briskly; the result should be almost crumbly. Mold biscuits three inches across and a quarter of an inch thick, place in a hot greased pan, and bake before a hot fire. The result is a thoroughly cooked, close-grained, crisp biscuit.

Corn pone is made in the same manner with cornmeal as the basis.

Flapjohn

Flapjack flour is mixed with water simply; but you will find that a tablespoonful of sugar not only adds to the flavor, but causes it to brown crisper. It is equally good baked in loaves. The addition of an extra spoonful of sugar, two eggs (from your canned desiccated eggs), raisins and cinnamon makes a delicious camp cake. This is known as "flapjohn"—a sort of sublimated flapjack.

Puddings.—The general logic of a camp-baked pudding is this:

How to Make Puddings

You have first of all your base, which is generally of rice, cornmeal, or breakfast food previously boiled; second, your filling, which may be raisins, prunes, figs, or any other dried fruit; third, your sweetening, which is generally sugar, but may be syrup, honey, or saccharine tablets; fourth, your seasoning, which must be what you have—cinnamon, nutmeg, lemon, etc., and last, your coagulating material, which must be a small portion of your egg powder. With this general notion you can elaborate.

The portions of materials, inclusive of other chance possessions, the arrangement of the ingredients determines the naming of the product. Thus you can mix your fruit all through the pudding, or you can place it in layers between strata of the mixture.

As an example: Boil one-half cupful of rice with raisins, until soft, add one-half cupful of sugar, a half spoonful of cinnamon, and a tablespoonful of egg powder. Add water (water mixed with condensed milk, if you have it) until quite thin. Bake in moderate heat. Another: Into two cups of boiling water pour a half cup of cornmeal. Sprinkle it in slowly, and stir in order to prevent lumps. As soon as it thickens, which will be in half a minute, remove from the fire. Mix in a quarter cup of syrup, some figs which have been soaked, a spoonful of egg powder, milk if you have it, and the flavoring—if you happen to have tucked in a can of ginger, that is the best. The mixture should be thin. Bake before moderate fire.

I am not going on to elaborate a number of puddings by name; that is where the cook-books make their mistake. But with this logical basis, you will soon invent all sorts of delicious combinations. Some will be failures, no doubt; but after you get the knack you will be able to improvise on the least promising materials.

Experiment Freely in Cooking

Do not forget that mixing ingredients is always worth trying. A combination of rice and oatmeal boiled together does not sound very good, but it is delicious, and quite unlike either of its component parts. I instance it merely as an example of a dozen similar.

How to Make Tea

Tea.—The usual way of cooking tea is to pour the hot water on the leaves. If used immediately this is the proper way. When, however, as almost invariably happens about camp, the water is left standing on the leaves for some time, the tannin is extracted. This makes a sort of tea soup, at once bitter and unwholesome. A simple and easy way is to provide yourself with a piece of cheesecloth about six inches square. On the center drop your dose of dry tea leaves. Gather up the corners, and tie into a sort of loose bag. Pour the hot water over this, and at the end of five minutes fish out the bag. Untie it, shake loose the tea leaves, and tuck away until next time. The tea in the pot can then be saved for the late fisherman without fear of lining his stomach with leather. Also it is no trouble.

On Coffee

Coffee, too, is more often bad than good in the field. The usual method is to put a couple of handfuls in cold water, bring it to a boil, and then set it aside to settle. Sometimes it is good that way, and sometimes it isn't. A method that will always succeed, however, is as follows: Bend an ordinary piece of hay wire into the shape of a hoop, slightly larger than the mouth of your pot. On it sew a shallow cheesecloth bag. Put your ground coffee in the bag, suspend in the coffee pot, and pour the hot water through. If you like it extra strong, pour it through twice. The result is drip coffee, delicious, and without grounds. To clean the bag turn it inside out and pour water through. Then flatten the hay wire hoop slightly and tuck it away inside the pot with the cups.

Mush.—The ideal method of cooking mush is of course a double boiler and just the amount of water the cereal will take up. Over an open fire, that would result in a burned product and a caked kettle. The best way is to make it very thin at first, and to boil it down to the proper consistency.

Beans will boil more quickly if you add a pinch of soda. An exaggerated pinch, however, causes them to taste soapy, so beware. If the water boils too low, add more *hot* water, never cold; the latter toughens them. When soft smash them with a fork, add water, and cook with fat in the frying pan.

In the heat of the day's struggle

A Quick Meal

Hardtack.—A most delicious dish to be eaten immediately is made of pilot bread soaked soft, and then fried. The same cracker fried in olive oil, without being previously soaked, comes out crisp and brown, but without impaired transportability. When butter is scarce this is a fine way to treat them in preparation for a cold lunch by the way.

Macaroni should be plunged in boiling water, otherwise it gets tough. What remains should be baked in mixture with whatever else is left—whether meal, cereal, or vegetable.

Corn.—After you have eaten what you want of the warmed-up, mix what is left with a spoonful or so of sugar, some diluted milk, and a spoonful of egg powder. Bake it.

Salmon may be eaten cold, but is better hashed up with bread crumbs, well moistened, and baked before a hot fire.

Cook-Books

These are but a few general hints which you will elaborate on. The Price Baking Powder Co. publish gratis a "Mine and Ranch Cookery" which is practical. Also read Nessmuk's *Woodcraft.*

A LIST OF SOME OF THE DISHES POSSIBLE WITHOUT TOO MUCH TROUBLE FROM THE GRUB LIST GIVEN IN THE LAST CHAPTER

Grub List

1. Fried bacon
2. Fried ham
3. Broiled ham
4. Boiled ham
5. Plain bread
6. Biscuits
7. Johnny cake
8. Oatmeal or cereal muffins
9. Pancakes or flapjacks
10. Buckwheat bread
11. Corn pone
12. Unleavened bread
13. Spice cakes
14. Dumplings
15. Boston brown bread
16. Brown bread gems
17. Boiled hominy
18. Fried hominy
19. Hominy pudding
20. Indian puddings (three or four sorts)
21. Cereal puddings (three or four sorts)
22. Oatmeal mush
23. Oatmeal and rice mush
24. Fried mush.
25. Boiled rice
26. Rice and raisins
27. Rice cakes
28. Rice biscuits
29. Rice pudding
30. Tea

31. Coffee
32. Baked potatoes
33. Boiled potatoes
34. Mashed potatoes
35. Fried potatoes
36. Boiled onions
37. Fried onions
38. Stewed fruits
39. Boiled beans
40. Fried beans
41. Baked beans
42. Fried hardtack
43. Boiled macaroni
44. Baked macaroni
45. Corn
46. Corn fritters
47. Corn pudding
48. Succotash
49. Baked salmon
50. Baked corned beef
51. Fried corned beef
52. Omelet
53. Scrambled eggs
54. Soup (several kinds)
55. Beans
56. Julienne, boiled or fried.

This leaves out of account the various hybrid mixtures of "what is left," and the meal and fish dishes in a good sporting country. As a matter of fact mixtures generally bake better than they boil.

CHAPTER IX

HORSE OUTFITS

Riding Saddles

WE have now finished the detailing of your wear and food. There remains still the problem of how you and it are to be transported. You may travel through the wilderness by land or by water. In the former case you will either go afoot or on horseback; in the latter you will use a canoe. Let us now consider in detail the equipments necessary for these different sorts of travel.

Sawbuck Saddle.

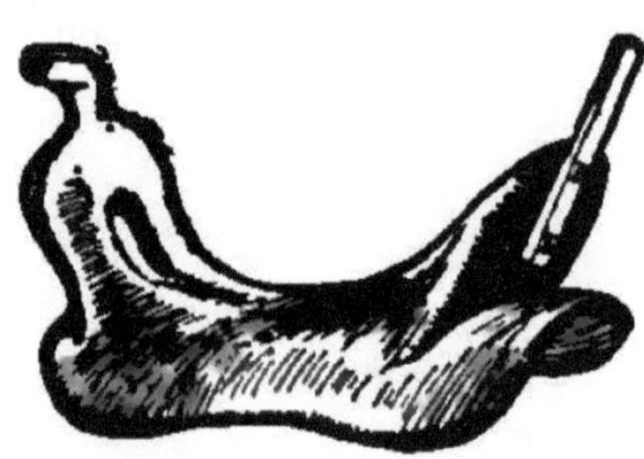

Riding Saddle.

You will find the Mexican or cowboy saddle the only really handy riding saddle. I am fully aware of the merits of the McClellan and army saddles, but they lack what seems to me one absolute essential, and that is the pommel or horn. By wrapping your rope about the latter you can lead reluctant horses, pull firewood to camp, extract bogged animals, and rope shy stock. Without it you are practically helpless in such circumstances. The only advantage claimed for the army saddle is its lightness. The difference in weight between it and the cowboy saddle need not be so marked as is ordinarily the case. A stock saddle, used daily in roping heavy cows, weighs quite properly from thirty-five to fifty pounds. The same saddle, of lighter leather throughout, made by a conscientious man, need weigh but twenty-five or thirty, and will still be strong and durable enough for all ordinary use. My own weighs but twenty-five pounds, and has seen some very hard service.

Stirrups

The stirrup leathers are best double, and should be laced, never buckled. In fact the logic of a wilderness saddle should be that it can be mended in any part with thongs. The stirrups themselves should have light hood tapaderos, or coverings. They will help in tearing through brush, will protect your toes, and will keep your feet dry in case of rain. I prefer the round rather than the square skirts.

Cinches

In a cow country you will hear many and heated discussions over the relative merits of the single broad cinch crossing rather far back; and the double cinches, one just behind the shoulder and the other on the curve of the belly. The double cinch is universally used by Wyoming and Arizona cowmen; and the "center fire" by Californians and Mexicans—and both with equally heated partisanship. Certainly as it would be difficult to say which are the better horsemen, so it would be unwise to attempt here a dogmatic settlement of the controversy.

Proper Way of Arranging Straps on Holster and Saddle.

Saddle Holster—Usual Arrangement of Straps.

How to Attach the Cinch

For ordinary mountain travel, however, I think there can be no doubt that the double cinch is the better. It is less likely to slip forward or back on steep hills; it need not be so tightly cinched as the "center fire," and can be adjusted, according to which you draw the tighter, for up or down hill. The front cinch should be made of hair. I have found that the usual cord cinches are apt to wear sores just back of the shoulder. Webbing makes a good back cinch. The handiest rig for attaching them is that used by the Texan and Wyoming cowmen. It is a heavy oiled latigo strap, punched with buckle holes, passing through a cinch ring supplied with a large buckle tongue. You can reach over and pull it up a hole or so without dismounting. It differs from an ordinary buckle only in that, in case the rig breaks, the strap can still be fastened like an ordinary latigo in the diamond knot.

Saddle Bags and Saddle Blankets

On the right-hand side of your pommel will be a strap and buckle for your riata. A pair of detachable leather saddle bags are handy. The saddle blanket should be thick and of first quality; and should be surmounted by a "corona" to prevent wrinkling under the slight movement of the saddle.

Quirts

A heavy quirt is indispensable, both for your own mount, if he prove refractory, but also for the persuasion of the pack horse.

Sling Shots

When with a large outfit, however, I always carry a pea shooter or sling shot. With it a man can spot a straying animal at considerable distance, generally much to the truant's astonishment. After a little it will rarely be necessary to shoot; a mere snapping of the rubbers will bring every horse into line.

Bridles

The handiest and best rig for a riding bridle can be made out of an ordinary halter. Have your harness maker fasten a snap hook to either side and just above the corners of the horse's mouth. When you start in the morning you snap your bit and reins to the hooks. When you arrive in the evening you simply unsnap the bit, and leave the halter on.

Riatas and Spurs

Rope and spurs will be necessary. I prefer the Mexican grass rope with a brass honda to the rawhide riata, because I am used to it. I once used a linen rope with weighted honda that was soft and threw well. The spurs will be of good steel, of the cowboy pattern, with blunt rowels. The smaller spurs are not so easy to reach a small horse with, and are apt to overdo the matter when they do. The wide spur leathers are to protect the boot from chafing on the stirrups.

Scabbards

There remains only your rifle to attend to. The usual scabbard is invariably slung too far forward. I always move the sling strap as near the mouth of the scabbard as it will go. The other sling strap I detach from the scabbard and hang loopwise from the back latigo-ring. Then I thrust the muzzle of the scabbarded rifle between the stirrup leathers and through this loop, hang the forward sling strap over the pommel—and there I am! The advantage is that I can remove rifle and scabbard without unbuckling any straps. The gun should hang on the left side of the horse so that after dismounting you need not walk around him to get it. A little experiment will show you how near the horizontal you can sling it without danger of its jarring out.

Pack Outfits

So much for your own riding horse. The pack outfit consists of the pack saddle, with the apparatus to keep it firm; its padding; the kyacks, or alforjas—sacks to sling on either side; and the lash rope and cinch with which to throw the hitches.

Pack Saddles

The almost invariable type of pack saddle is the sawbuck. If it is bought with especial reference to the animal it is to be used on, it is undoubtedly the best. But nothing will more quickly gouge a hole in a horse's back than a saddle too narrow or too wide for his especial anatomy. A saddle of this sort bolted together can be taken apart for easier transportation by baggage or express.

Another and very good type of pack rig is that made from an old riding saddle. The stirrup rigging is removed, and an upright spike bolted strongly to the cantle. The loops of the kyacks are to be hung over the horn and this spike. Such a saddle is apt to be easy on a horse's back, but is after all merely a make-shift for a properly constructed sawbuck.

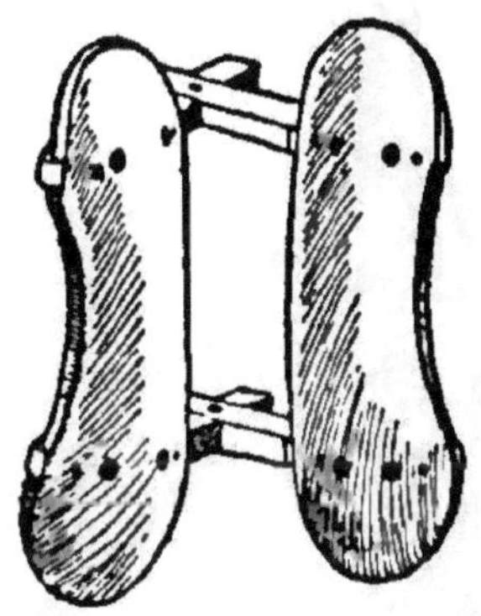

Under Side of Pack Saddles.

Shape of Collar Pad—for Pack Saddles.

Aparejos

I shall only mention the aparejos. This rig is used for freighting boxes and odd-shaped bundles. It is practically nothing but a heavy pad, and is used without kyacks. You will probably never be called upon to use it; but in another chapter I will describe one "sling" in order that you may be forearmed against contingencies.

Pads

We will assume that you are possessed of a good sawbuck saddle of the right size for your pack animal. It will have the double cinch rig. To the under surfaces tack firmly two ordinary collar-pads by way of softening. Beneath them you will use two blankets, each as heavy as the one you place under your riding saddle. This abundance is necessary because a pack "rides dead"—that is, does not favor the horse as does a living rider. By way of warning, however, too much is almost as bad as too little.

Breasting and Breeching

The almost universal saddle rigging in use the West over is a breast strap of webbing fastened at the forward points of the saddle, and a breech strap fastened to the back points of the saddle, with guy lines running from the top to prevent its falling too far down the horse's legs. This, with the double cinch, works fairly well. Its main trouble is that the breech strap is apt to work up under the horse's tail, and the breast strap is likely to shut off his wind at the throat.

The Britten Pack Rig

Mr. Ernest Britten, a mountaineer in the Sierras, has, however, invented a rig which in the nicety of its compensations, and the accuracy of its adjustments is perfection. Every one becomes a convert, and hastens to alter his own outfit.

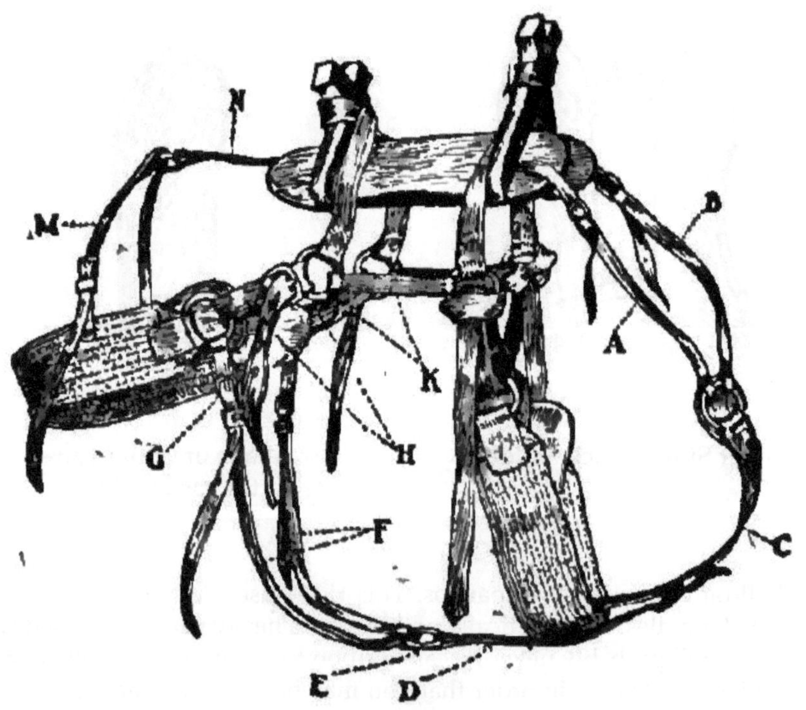

Mr. Ernest Britten's Pack Rig.

The breasting is a strap (*a*) running from the point of the saddle to a padded ring in the middle of the chest. Thence another strap (*b*) runs to the point of the saddle on the other side, where it buckles. A third strap (*c*) in the shape of a loop goes between the fore legs and around the front cinch.

The Britten Pack Rig

The breeching is somewhat more complicated. I think, however, with a few rivets, straps, and buckles you will be able to alter your own saddle in half an hour.

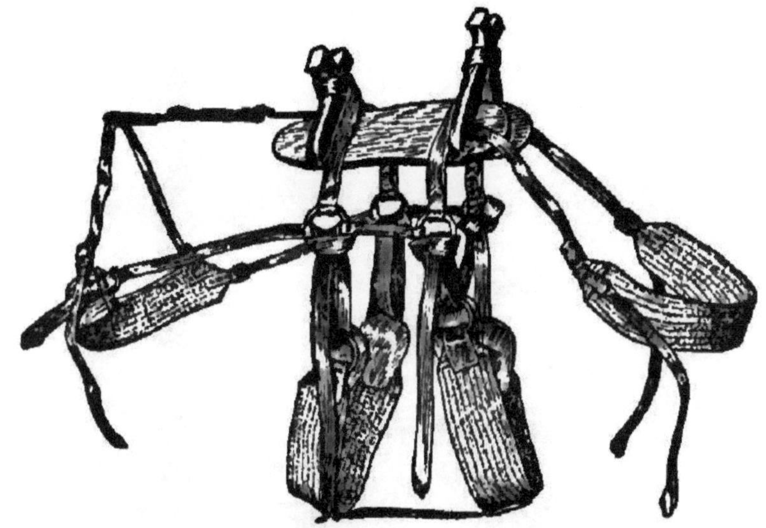

Ordinary and Inferior Pack Rig Usually Employed.

The back cinch you remove. A short strap (*d*), riveted to the middle of the front cinch, passes back six inches to a ring (*e*). This ring will rest on the middle of the belly. From the ring two other straps (*ff*) ascend diagonally to the buckles (*g*) in the ends of the breeching. From the ends of the breeching other straps (*h*) attach to what would be the back cinch ring (*k*). That constitutes the breeching rig. It is held up by a long strap (*m*) passing from one side to the other over the horse's rump through a ring on top. The ring is attached to the saddle by a short strap (*n*).

Such a rig prevents the breeching from riding up or dropping down; it gives the horse all his wind going up hill, but holds firmly going down; when one part loosens, the other tightens; and the saddle cinch, except to keep the saddle from turning, is practically useless and can be left comparatively loose. I cannot too strongly recommend you, both for your horse's comfort and your own, to adopt this rigging.

Kyacks

The kyacks, as I have said, are two sacks to be slung one on each side of the horse. They are provided with loops by which to hang them over the sawbucks of the saddle, and a long strap passes from the outside of one across the saddle to a buckle on the outside of the other.

Nearing a crest and in sight of game

Undoubtedly the best are those made of rawhide. They weigh very little, will stand all sorts of hard usage, hold the pack rope well, are so stiff that they well protect the contents, and are so hard that miscellaneous sharp-cornered utensils may be packed in them without fear of injury either to them or the animal. They are made by lacing wet hides, hair out, neatly and squarely over one of the wooden boxes built to pack two five gallon oil cans. A round hardwood stick is sewn along the top on one side—to this the sling straps are to be attached. After the hide has dried hard, the wooden box is removed.

Only one possible objection can be urged against rawhide kyacks; if you are traveling much by railroad, they are exceedingly awkward to ship. For that purpose they are better made of canvas.

Canvas Kyacks

Lash Ropes

Many canvas kyacks are on the market, and most of them are worthless. It is astonishing how many knocks they are called on to receive and how soon the abrasion of rocks and trees will begin to wear them through. Avoid those made of light material. Avoid also those made in imitation of the rawhide with a stick along the top of one side to take the sling straps. In no time the ends of that stick will punch through. The best sort are constructed of OO canvas. The top is made of a half-inch rope sewn firmly to the hem all around. The sling straps are long, and riveted firmly. The ends are reinforced with leather. Such kyacks will give you good service and last you a long time. When you wish to express them, you pack your saddle and saddle blankets in one, telescope the other over it, and tie up the bundle with the lash rope. The lash rope is important, for you will have to handle it much, and a three months' trip with a poor one would lose you your immortal soul. Most articles on the subject advise thirty-three feet. That is long enough for the diamond hitch and for other hitches with a very small top pack, but it will not do for many valuable hitches on a bulky pack. Forty feet is nearer the ticket. The best is a manila half inch or five-eighth inch. If you boil it before starting out, you will find it soft to handle. The boiling does not impair its strength. Parenthetically: do not become over-enthusiastic and boil your riata, or you will make it aggravatingly kinky. Cotton rope is all right, but apt to be stiff. I once used a linen rope; it proved to be soft, strong, and held well, but I have never been able to find another.

Cinch Hooks

The cinch hook sold with the outfit is sawn into shape and strengthened with a bolt. If you will go out into the nearest oak grove, however, you can cut yourself a natural hook which will last longer and hold much better. The illustration shows the method of attaching such a hook.

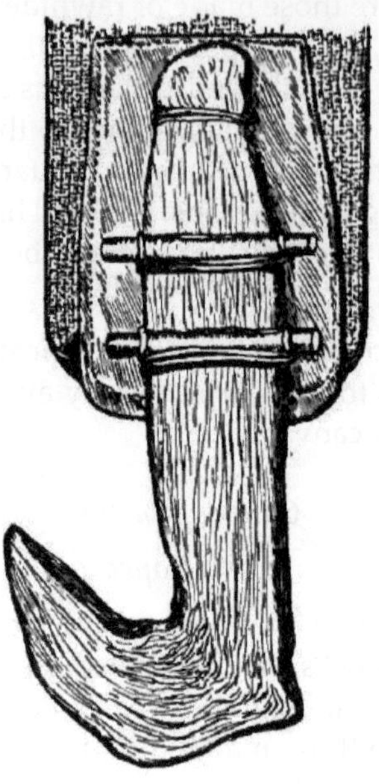

Natural Cinch Hook of Oak.

Picket Ropes

So you have your horses ready for their burdens. Picket ropes should be of half-inch rope and about 50 feet long. The bell for the bell horse should be a loud one, with distinctive note not easily blended with natural sounds, and attached to a broad strap with safety buckle.

A—Wash Leather. *C—Steel Ring.*
B—Heavy Leather. *D—Buckle.*
E—Swivel.

Hobbles—Wrong (Upper) and Right Sort.

Hobbles

Hobbles are of two patterns. Both consist of heavy leather straps to buckle around either front leg and connected by two links and a swivel. In one the strap passes first through the ring to which the links are attached, and then to the buckle. The other buckles first, and then the end is carried through the ring. You will find the first mentioned a decided nuisance, especially on a wet or frosty morning, for the leather tends to atrophy in a certain position from which numbed fingers have more than a little difficulty in dislodging it. The latter, however, are comparatively easy to undo.

Hobbles should be lined. I have experimented with various materials, including the much lauded sheepskin with the wool on. The latter when wet chafes as much as raw leather, and when frozen is about as valuable as a wood rasp. The best lining is a piece of soft wash leather at least two inches wider than the hobble straps.

How to Attach Hobbles

With most horses it is sufficient to strap a pair of these around the forelegs and above the fetlocks. A gentle animal can be trusted with them fastened below.

But many horses by dint of practice or plain native cussedness can hop along with hobbles nearly as fast as they could foot-free, and a lot too fast for you to catch them single handed. Such an animal is an unmitigated bother. Of course if there is good staking you can picket him out; but quite likely he is unused to the picket rope, or the feed is scant.

Side Lines

In that case it may be that side lines—which are simply hobbles by which a hind foot and a fore foot are shackled—may work. I have had pretty good success by fastening a short heavy chain to one fore leg. As long as the animal fed quietly, he was all right, but an attempt at galloping or trotting swung the chain sufficiently to rap him sharply across the shins.

Very good hobbles can be made from a single strand unraveled from a large rope, doubled once to make a loop for one leg, twisted strongly, the two ends brought around the other leg and then thrust through the fibers. This is the sort used generally by cowboys. They are soft and easily carried, but soon wear out.

CHAPTER X
HORSE PACKS

Generalities

ALMOST any one can put together a comparatively well made back pack, and very slight practice will enable a beginner to load a canoe. But the packing of a horse or mule is another matter. The burden must be properly weighted, properly balanced, properly adjusted, and properly tied on. That means practice and considerable knowledge.

To the average wilderness traveler the possession of a pack saddle and canvas kyacks simplifies the problem considerably. If you were to engage in packing as a business, wherein probably you would be called on to handle packages of all shapes and sizes, however, you would be compelled to discard your kyacks in favor of a sling made of rope. And again it might very well happen that some time or another you might be called on to transport your plunder without appliances on an animal caught up from the pasture. For this reason you must further know how to hitch a pack securely to a naked horse.

In this brief résumé of possibilities you can see it is necessary that you know at least three methods of throwing a lash rope—a hitch to hold your top pack and kyacks, a sling to support your boxes on the aparejos, and a hitch for the naked horse. But in addition it will be desirable to understand other hitches adapted to different exigencies of bulky top packs, knobby kyacks and the like. One hitch might hold these all well enough, but the especial hitch is better.

Pack Models

The detailment of processes by diagram must necessarily be rather dull reading. It can be made interesting by an attempt to follow out in actual practice the hitches described. For this purpose you do not need a full-size outfit. A pair of towels folded compactly, tied together, and thrown one each side over a bit of stove wood to represent the horse makes a good pack, while a string with a bent nail for cinch hook will do as lash rope. With these you can follow out each detail.

Saddling the Horse

First of all you must be very careful to get your saddle blankets on smooth and without wrinkles. Hoist the saddle into place, then lift it slightly and loosen the blanket along the length of the backbone, so that the weight of the pack will not bind the blanket tight across the horse's back. In cinching up, be sure you know your animal; some puff themselves out so that in five minutes the cinch will hang loose. Fasten your latigo or cinch straps to the *lower* ring. Thus you can get at it even when the pack is in place.

Packing the Kyacks

Distribute the weight carefully between the kyacks. "Heft" them again and again. The least preponderance on one side will cause a saddle to sag in that direction; that in turn will bring pressure to bear on the opposite side of the withers, and that will surely chafe to a sore. Then you are in trouble.

When you are quite sure the kyacks weigh alike, get your companion to hang one on the pack saddle, at the same time you hook the straps of the other. If you try to do it by yourself you must leave one hanging while you pick up the other, thus running a good risk of twisting the saddle.

Top Packs

Your top pack you will build as the occasion demands. In general, try to make it as low as possible and to get your blankets on top where the pack rope "bites." The strap connecting the kyacks is then buckled. Over all you will throw the canvas tarpaulin that you use to sleep on. Tuck it in back and front to exclude dust. It is now ready for the pack rope.

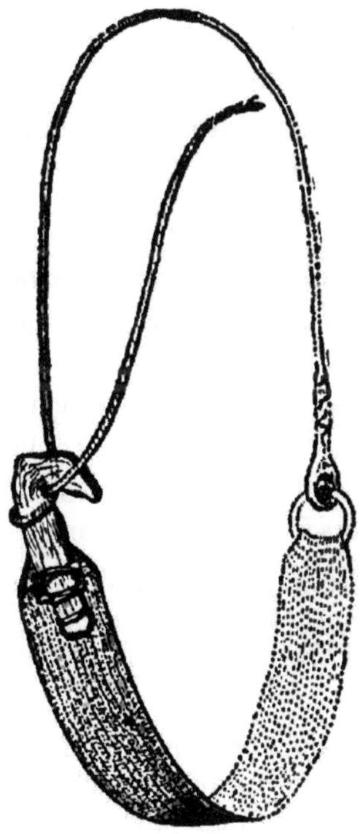

The Jam Hitch.

Jam Hitch

1. *The Jam Hitch.*—All hitches possess one thing in common—the rope passes around the horse and through the cinch hook. The first pull is to tighten that cinch. Afterward other maneuvers are attempted. Now ordinarily the packer pulls tight his cinch, and then in the further throwing of the hitch he depends on holding his slack. It is a very difficult thing to do. With the jam hitch, however, the necessity is obviated. The beauty of it is that the rope renders freely one way—the way you are pulling—but will not give a hair the other—the direction of loosening. So you may heave up the cinch as tightly as you please, then drop the rope and go on about your packing perfectly sure that nothing is going to slip back on you.

The rope passes once around the shank of the hook, and then through the jaw (see diagram). Be sure to get it around the shank and not the curve. Simplicity itself; and yet I have seen very few packers who know of it.

The Diamond Hitch

2. *The Diamond Hitch.*—I suppose the diamond in one form or another is more used than any other. Its merit is its adaptability to different shapes and sizes of package—in fact it is the only hitch good for aparejo packing—its great flattening power, and the fact that it rivets the pack to the horse's sides. If you are to learn but one hitch, this will be the best for you, although certain others, as I shall explain under their proper captions, are better adapted to certain circumstances.

The diamond hitch is also much discussed. I have heard more arguments over it than over the Japanese war or original sin.

"That thing a diamond hitch!" shrieks a son of the foothills to a son of the alkali. "Go to! Looks more like a game of cat's cradle. Now *this* is the real way to throw a diamond."

Colorado Versus Arizona

Certain pacifically inclined individuals have attempted to quell the trouble by a differentiation of nomenclature. Thus one can throw a number of diamond hitches, provided one is catholically minded—such as the "Colorado diamond," the "Arizona diamond," and others. The attempt at peace has failed.

"Oh, yes," says the son of the alkali as he watches the attempts of the son of the foothills. "That's the *Colorado* diamond," as one would say that is a *paste* jewel.

The joke of it is that the results are about the same. Most of the variation consists in the manner of throwing. It is as though the discussion were whether the trigger should be pulled with the fore, middle, or both fingers. After all, the bullet would go anyway.

I describe here the single diamond, as thrown in the Sierra Nevadas, and the double diamond as used by government freight packers in many parts of the Rockies. The former is a handy one-man hitch. The latter can be used by one man, but is easier with two.

A downward journey

The Single Diamond

Throw the pack cinch (*a*) over the top of the pack, retaining the loose end of the rope. If your horse is bad, reach under him with a stick to draw the cinch within reach of your hand until you hold it and the loose end both on the same side of the animal. Hook it through the hook (*a*, Fig. II) and bring up along the pack. Thrust the bight (*a*, Fig. III) of the loose rope under the rope (*b*); the back over and again under to form a loop. The points (*c-c*) at which the loose rope goes around the pack rope can be made wide apart or close together, according to the size of the diamond required (Fig. V). With a soft top-pack requiring flattening, the diamond should be large; with heavy side pack, smaller.

Now go around to the other side of the animal. Pass the loose end (*d*, Fig. III) back, under the alforjas, forward and through the loop from below as shown by the arrows of direction in Fig. IV.

You are now ready to begin tightening. First pull your cinch tight by means of what was the loose end (*b*) in Fig. II. Place one foot against the animal and *heave*, good and plenty. Take up the slack by running over both ends of the loop (*c-c* Fig. III). When you have done this, go around the other side. There take up the slack on *b-b* Fig. IV. With all there is in you pull the loose end (*c*, Fig. IV) in the direction of the horse's body, toward his head. Brace your foot against the kyacks. It will sag the whole hitch toward the front of the pack, but don't mind that: the defect will be remedied in a moment.

Next, still holding the slack (Fig. V), carry the loose end around the bottom of the alforjas and under the original main pack rope (*c*). Now pull again along the direction of the horse's body, but this time toward his tail. The strain will bend the pack rope (*c*), heretofore straight across, back to form the diamond. It will likewise drag back to its original position amidships in the pack the entire hitch, which, you will remember, was drawn too far forward by your previous pull toward the horse's head. Thus the last pull tightens the entire pack, clamps it down, secures it immovably, which is the main recommendation and beautiful feature of the diamond hitch.

The Double Diamond

The double diamond is a much more complicated affair. Begin by throwing the cinch under, not over the horse. Let it lie there. Lay the end of the rope (*a*) lengthwise of the horse across one side the top of the pack (Fig. 1). Experience will teach you just how big to leave loop (*b*). Throw loop (*b*) over top of pack (Fig. 2). Reverse loop *a* (Fig. 2) by turning it from left to right (Fig. 3). Pass loop (*a*) around front and back of kyack, and end of rope *d* over rope *c*, and under rope *d*. Pass around the horse and hook the cinch hook in loop (*e*).

This forms another loop (*a*, Fig. 4), which must be extended to the proper size and passed around the kyack on the other side (Fig. 5). Now tighten the cinch, pull up the slack, giving strong heaves where the hitch pulls forward or back along the left of the horse, ending with a last tightener at the end (*b*, Fig. 5). The end is then carried back under the kyack and fastened.

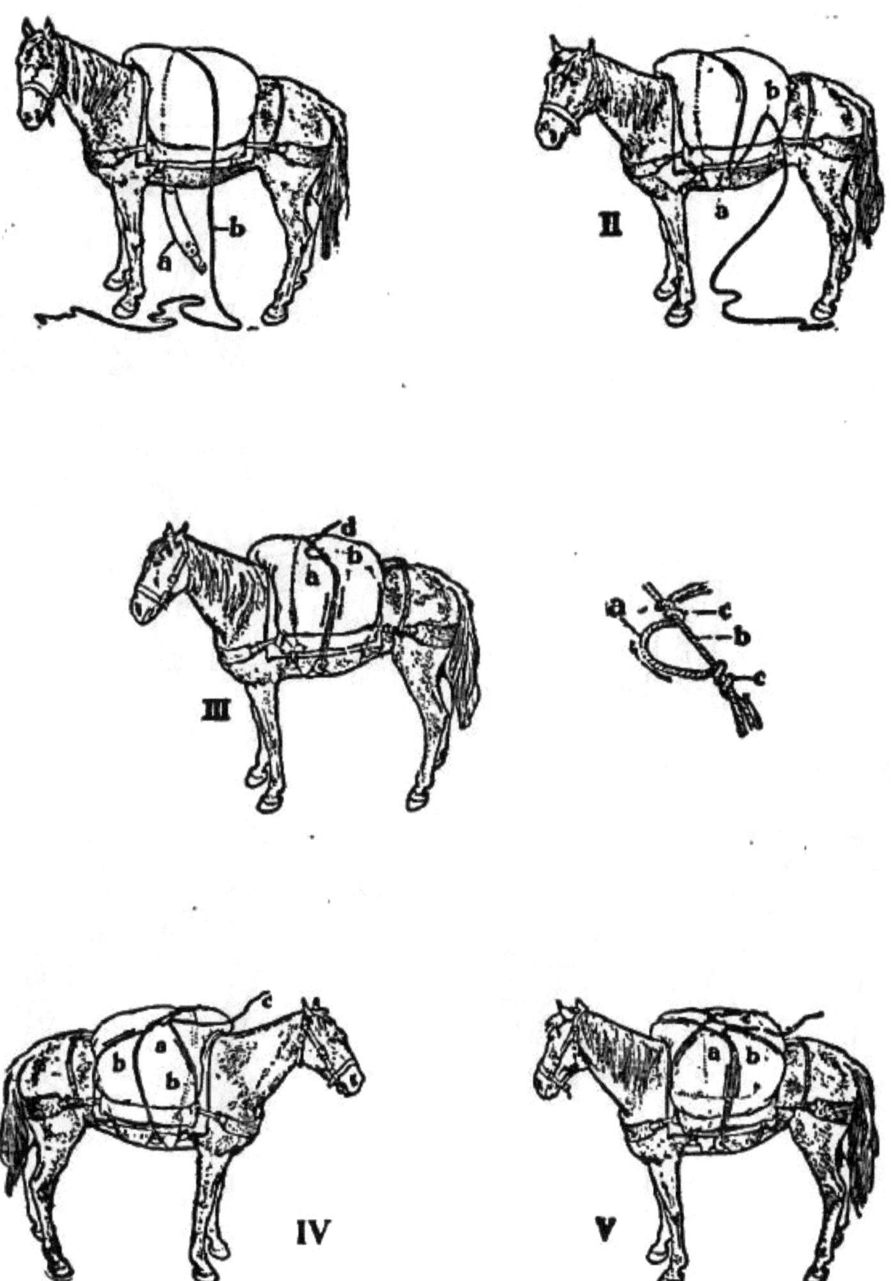

The Single Diamond.

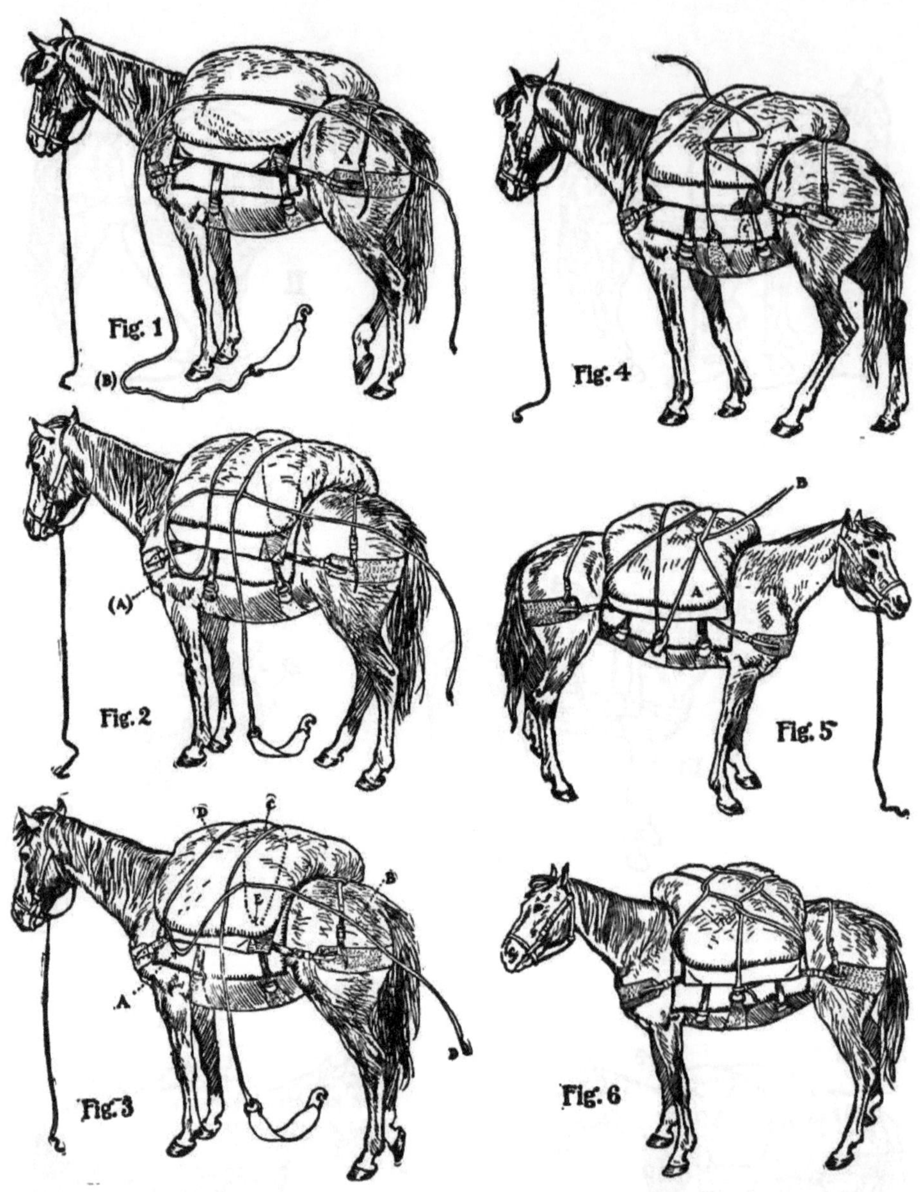

The Double Diamond. **The Double Diamond.**

The Square Hitch

3. *The Square Hitch* is easily and quickly thrown, and is a very good fair-weather lash. In conjunction with half hitches, as later explained, it makes a good hitch for a bucking horse. For a very bulky pack it is excellent in that it binds in so many places. It is thrown as follows:

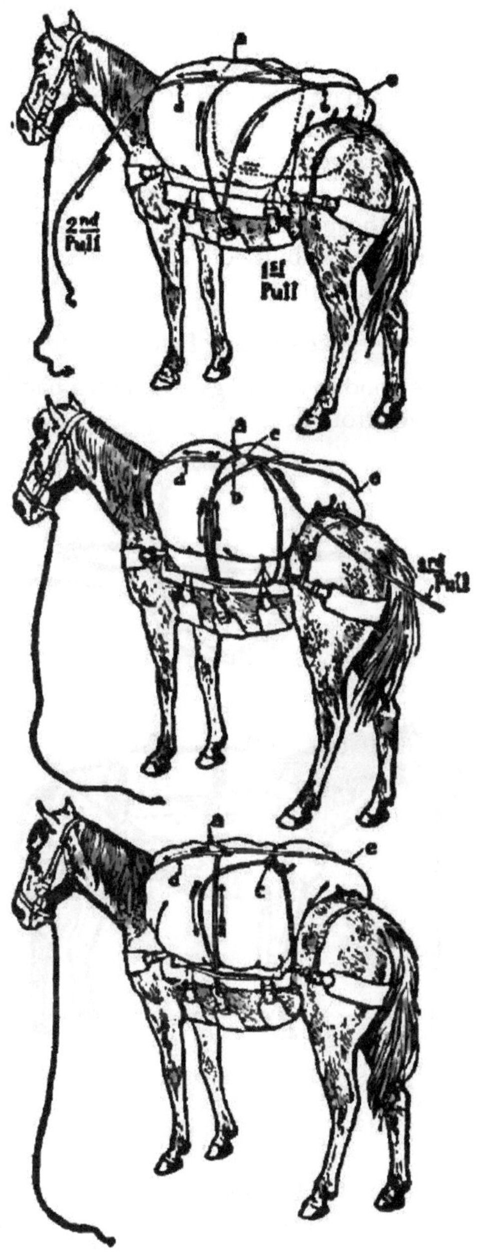

The Square Hitch.

Throw the cinch hook over the pack, and cinch tight with the jam hitch before described. Lead the end across the horse, around the back of kyack on the other side, underneath it, and up over at *a*. The end here passes beneath at *b*. You will find that you can, when you cinch up at first, throw a loose loop over the pack comprising the bight *bed*, so as to leave your loose end at *d*. Then place the loop *bed* around the kyack. A moment's study of the diagram will show you what I mean, and will also convince you that much is gained by not having to pass rope (*a*) underneath at *b*. Now pull hard on loose end at *d*, taking care to exert your power lengthwise of the horse. Pass the line under the alforjas toward the rear, up over the pack and under the original rope at *c*. Pull on the loose end, this time exerting the power toward the rear. You cannot put too much strength into the three tightening pulls: (1) in cinching through the cinch hook; (2) the pull forward; (3) the pull back. On them depends the stability of your pack. Double back the loose end and fasten it. This is a very quick hitch.

The Bucking Hitch

4. *The Bucking Hitch* is good to tie things down on a bad horse, but it is otherwise useless to take so much trouble.

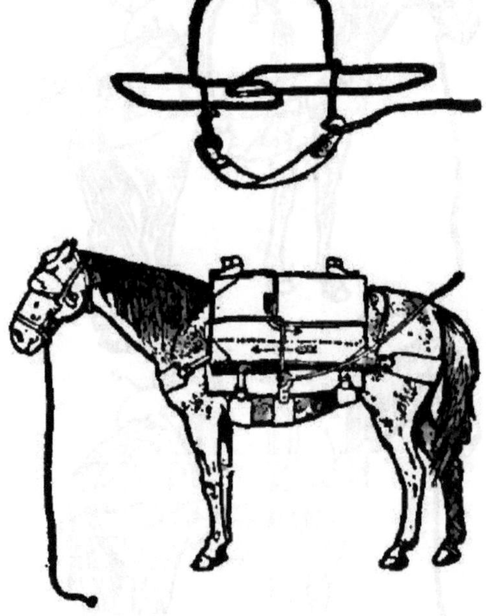

The Bucking Hitch.

Pass the pack rope around the kyacks on one side, and over itself. This forms a half hitch, below which hangs the cinch. Lead the pack rope over the top of the pack, around the other kyack, and through to form another half hitch. Cinch up, and throw either the single diamond or the square hitch. The combination will clamp the kyacks as firmly as anything can.

The Miner's Hitch

5. *The Miner's Hitch.*—This hitch is very much on the same principle, but is valuable when you happen to be provided with only a short rope, or a cinch with

two rings, instead of a ring and a hook.

The Miner's Hitch.

Take your rope—with the cinch unattached—by the middle and throw it across the pack. Make a half hitch over either kyack. These half hitches, instead of running around the sides of the kyacks, as in the last hitch, should run around the top, bottom, and ends (see diagram). Thrust bight (*b*) through cinch ring, and end (*a*) through the bight. Do the same thing on the other side. Make fast end *a* at *c*, and end *d* at *e*, cinching up strongly on the bights that come through the cinch rings.

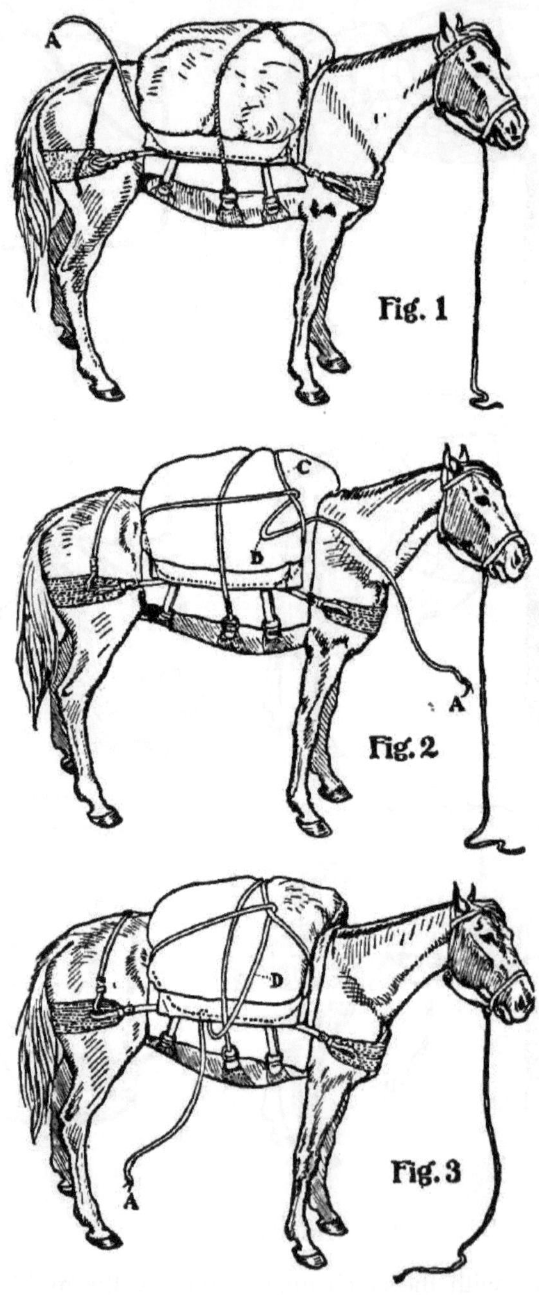

The Lone Packer Hitch.

The Lone Packer Hitch

6. *The Lone Packer or Basco Hitch.*—This is a valuable hitch when the kyacks are heavy or knobby, because the last pull lifts them away from the horse's sides. It requires at least forty feet of rope. I use it a great deal.

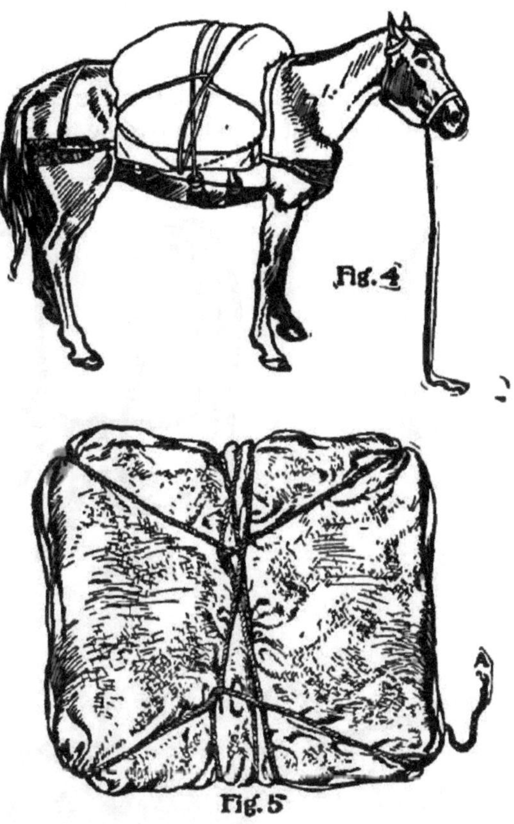

The Lone Packer Hitch.

Cinch up with the jam hitch as usual. Throw the end of the rope across the horse, under the forward end of the kyack on the far side, beneath it and up over the rear end of the kyack. The rope in all other hitches binds against the bottom of the kyacks; but in this it should pass between the kyack and the horse's side (Fig. 1). Now bring a bight in loose end (*a*) forward *over* rope (*c*), and thrust it through *under* rope (*c*) from front to back (Fig. 2). Be sure to get this right. Hold bight (*b*) with left hand where it is, and with the other slide end (*a*) down along rope (*c*) until beneath the kyacks (Fig. 3). Seize rope at *d* and pull hard directly back; then pull cinchwise on *a*. The first pull tightens the pack; the second lifts the kyacks. Carry end (*a*) across the pack and repeat on the other side. Fasten finally anywhere on top. Fig. 4 shows one side completed, with rope thrown across ready for the other side. Fig. 5 is a view from above of the hitch, completed except for the fastening of end (*a*).

A Modification

In case you have eggs or glassware to pack, spread your tarp on the horse twice as long as usual. Cinch up with the jam hitch, lay your eggs, etc., atop the rope; fold back the canvas to cover the whole, and then throw the lone packer, placing one rope each side the package (Figs. 6 and 7).

The Squaw Hitch

7. *The Squaw Hitch.*—Often it may happen that you find yourself possessed of a rope and a horse, but nothing else. It is quite possible to pack your equipment with only these simple auxiliaries.

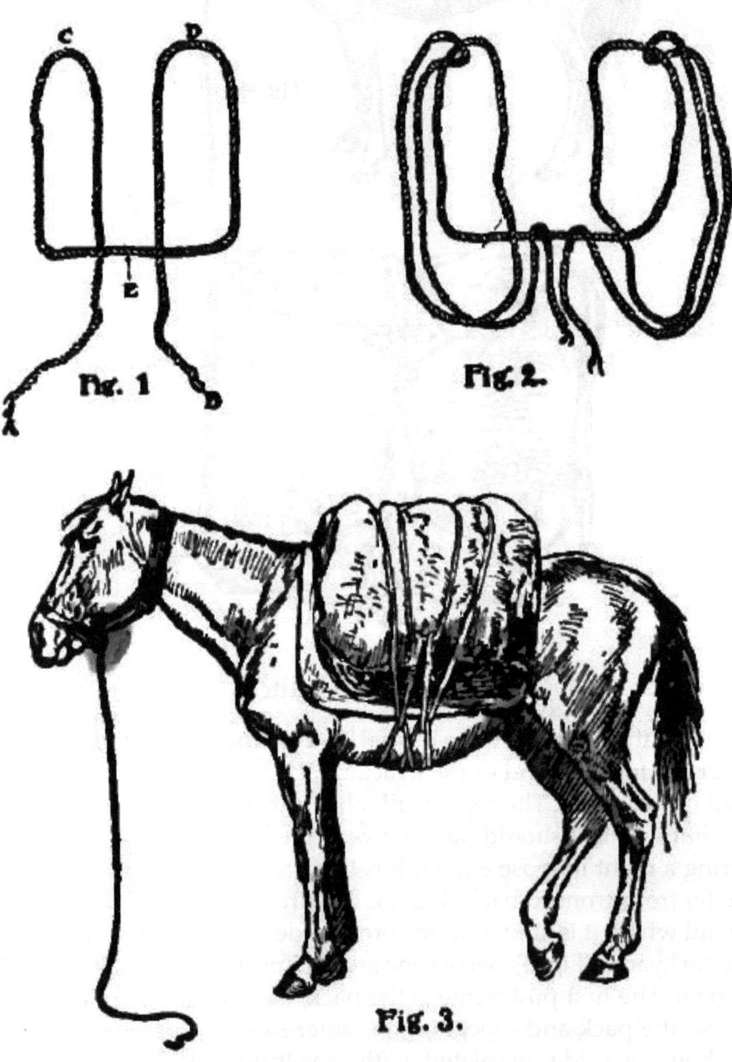

The Squaw Hitch.

Lay your tarp on the ground fully spread. On half of it pack your effects, striving always to keep them as flat and smooth as possible. Fold the other half of the canvas to cover the pack. Lay this thick mattress-like affair across the horse's bare back, and proceed to throw the squaw hitch as follows:

Throw a double bight across the top of the pack (Fig. 1). Pass end *a* under the horse and through loop *c;* and end *b* under the horse and through loop (*d*). Take both *a* and *b* directly back under the horse again, in the opposite direction, of course, and pass both through loop (*e*). Now cinch up on the two ends and fasten.

Sling

8. *Sling No. 1.*—When you possess no kyacks, but have some sort of pack saddle, it is necessary to improvise a sling.

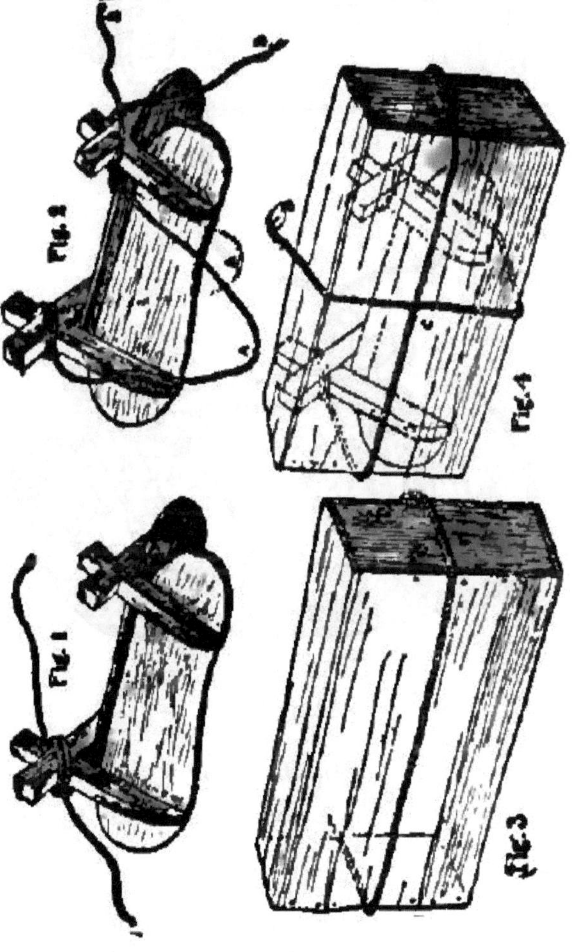

Sling No. 1.

Fasten the middle of your rope by means of two half hitches to the front of the pack saddle (Fig. 1). Throw the ends (*b, b*) crossed as shown in Fig. 2. Place the box or sack in bight (*a*), passing the rope around the outside and the ends, as in Fig. 3. The end of the sack should be just even with the front of the pack saddle. If you bring it too far forward the front of the sling will sag. Pass the end (*b*) underneath the sack or burden, across its middle, and over the top of the saddle. When the other side is similarly laden, the ends (*b, b*) may be tied together at the top; or if they are long enough, may be fastened at *c* (Fig. 4).

Sling No. 2.

Another Sling

9. *Sling No. 2.*—Another sling is sometimes handy for long bundles, and is made as follows:

Fasten the rope by the middle as explained in the last. Fasten ends (*b, b*) to the rear horn or to each other (see diagram). Leave the bights of the rope (*a, a*) of sufficient length so they can be looped around the burden and over the horns. This sling is useful only on a regular pack saddle, while the other really does not need the rear pommel at all, as the ropes can be crossed without it.

The Saddle Hitch

10. *The Saddle Hitch.*—There remains now the possibility, or let us hope probability, that you may some day wish to pack a deer on your riding saddle, or perhaps bring in a sack of grain or some such matter.

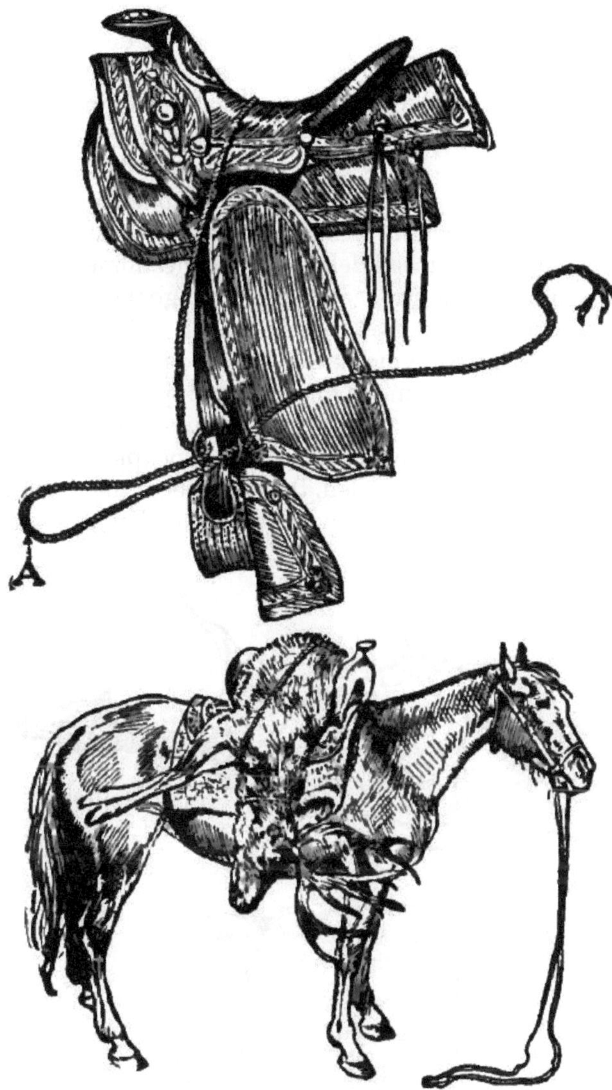

The Saddle Hitch.

Throw the rope across the seat of the saddle, leaving long ends on both sides. Lay your deer aboard, crosswise. Thrust a bight (*a*) of one end through your cinch ring, and pass the loop thus formed around the deer's neck (Fig. 1). Repeat on the other side, bringing the loop there about his haunch. Cinch up the two ends of the rope, and tie them on top.

How to Pack Fragile Stuff

The great point in throwing any hitch is to keep the rope taut. To do this, pay no attention to your free end, but clamp down firmly the fast end with your left hand until the right has made the next turn. Remember this; it is important. The least slip back of the slack you have gained is going to loosen that pack by ever so little; and then you can rely on the swing and knocks of the day's journey to do the rest. The horse rubs under a limb or against a big rock; the loosened rope scrapes off the top of the pack; something flops or rattles or falls—immediately that cayuse arches his back, lowers his head, and begins to buck. It is marvelous to what height the bowed back will send small articles catapult-wise into the air. First go the tarpaulin and blankets; then the duffle bags; then one by one the contents of the alforjas; finally, after they have been sufficiently lightened, the alforjas themselves in an abandoned parabola of debauched delight. In the meantime that horse, and all the others, has been running frantically all over the rough mountains, through the rocks, ravines, brush and forest trees. You have ridden recklessly trying to round them up, sweating, swearing, praying to the Red Gods that none of those indispensable animals is going to get lame in this insane hippodrome. Finally between you, you have succeeded in collecting and tying to trees all the culprits. Then you have to trail inch by inch along the track of the cyclone, picking up from where they have fallen, rolled, or been trampled, the contents of that pack down to the smallest. It will take you the rest of the day; and then you'll miss some. Oh, it pays to get your hitch on snug!

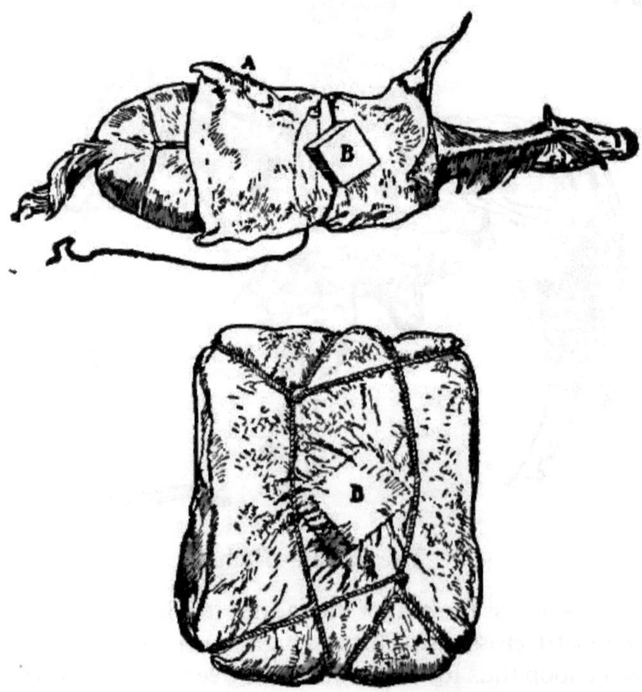

Illustrating How to Pack Eggs or Glassware.

The Result of Not Getting the Hitch on Snug.

The Tie Hitch

11. *The Tie Hitch.*—The hitches described are all I have ever had occasion to use, and will probably carry you through any emergencies that may be likely to arise. But perhaps many times during the day you are likely to want to stop the train for the purpose of some adjustments. Therefore you will attach your lead ropes in a manner easily to be thrown loose. Thrust the bight (*a*) of the lead rope beneath any part of the pack rope (*b, b*). Double back the bight (*d*) of the loose end (*c*) through the loop (*a*) thus formed. Tighten the knot by pulling tight on loop *d*. A sharp pull on *c* will free the entire lead rope.

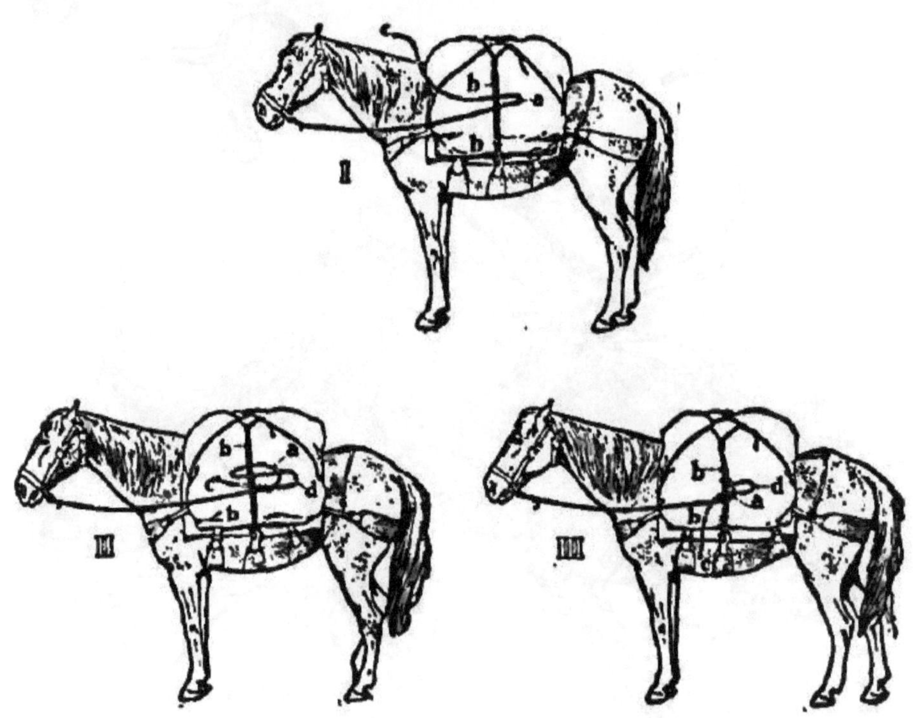

The Tie Hitch.

CHAPTER XI

HORSES, MULES, BURROS

Mules

A GOOD riding mule, when you can get him, and provided you intend to use him only for trail travel in the mountains, is about the best proposition. A mule is more sure-footed than a horse, and can subsist where a horse would starve. On the other hand he is not much good off a walk; never acquires the horse's interest in getting around stubborn stock, and is apt to be mean. None of these objections, however much they may influence your decision as to saddle animals, will have any weight against a pack beast. For the latter purpose the mule is unexcelled. But probably in the long run you will prefer to ride a horse.

Burros

Burros are an aggravation; and yet in some circumstances they are hard to beat. They are unbelievably slow, and unbelievably stubborn. When they get tired—or think they do—they stop, and urging merely confirms their decision to rest. You cannot hurry them. They hate water, and it is sometimes next to impossible to force them into a deep or swift stream. They are camp thieves, and will eat anything left within their reach. Still, they can live on sage-bush, go incredible periods without drinking, make their way through country impassible to any other hoofed animals excepting goats and sheep. Certain kinds of desert travel is impossible without them, and some sorts of high rough mountaineering is practicable only with their aid. At times you will be driven to the use of them. In such an emergency gird your soul with patience, and try to buy big ones.

Pack Mules

Pack mules are almost impossible to get, and are generally very high priced. A good pack mule does not mean any old mule that comes along. The animal should be rather small, chunkily built, gentle as to the heels and teeth, accustomed to carrying and taking care of a pack, trained to follow the saddle horses, and not inclined to stray from camp. Such perfection costs anywhere from seventy-five to one hundred and fifty dollars. It is worth the price to one who does much packing; but as perfectly adequate pack horses can be had for from twenty to forty dollars, and are easy to find, you will in all likelihood choose them.

Choosing a Horse

Now I know perfectly well that I can tell you nothing about choosing a horse. If you are a New Englander you will know all about the trade; if you are a New Yorker, you could give me points on every horse in the ring; if you are Middle West, you probably have read or worked or traded or raised more horses than I will ever ride. But in selecting a mountain horse, his mere points as a physical specimen are often little in his favor, while glaring defects may concern his usefulness hardly at all.

Western Horses

Never mind at first how the horse offered for your inspection looks. Examine him for blemishes later. You must first discover if he is sure-footed and courageous. An eastern horse would not last five minutes on a western trail. A western horse, no matter how accustomed to mountain work, is worse than useless if subject to ordinary horse-panics at suddenly rustling leaves, unexpected black stubs, and the like. He must attend to his footing, keep his eyes for the trail, and *be wise*. Next you must inquire if this steadiness carries over into other things. He must stand when left without hitching, and must be easy to catch. Often you will have to dismount for the purpose of clearing trail, helping the pack train, tightening ropes, or reconnoitering. At such junctures iron hitching posts are not always at hand. Nothing is more aggravating than the necessity of searching everywhere for a place to tie, or worse, to be forced to chase down and coax quiet a horse that has promptly decamped when left for a moment to himself. Nor does it add to your joy to get up at four for the purpose of making an early start, only to spend the extra hour filched from sleep in an attempt to catch some snorting fool horse.

The picture I have sketched looks to you somewhat like what is known as an "old cow," doesn't it? But in reality good horses of the quality named are not difficult to find. Equine intelligence is of a higher grade West than East, mainly because a western horse is all his life thrown on his own resources. It is perfectly possible to find a horse both handsome and spirited, which will nevertheless permit himself to be directly approached in pasture, and will stand until further orders on the trail.

An "Old Cow" of a Horse

But the point is that it is much better, oh, infinitely! to get an "old cow" than a horse without these qualities. The "old cow" will carry you, and will be there when wanted. That is the main thing in the mountains. While as for the other horse, no matter how well bred he is, how spirited, how well gaited, how handsome, how appealing in every way to a horseman's eye—he will be worse than no horse if you have to keep your hands on him, if he must be picketed at night, if he is likely to shy on a bad trail, if he may refuse to tackle a rough place or to swim a river.

In mid-day the shade of the pines is inviting

A Handsome Horse Not Necessary

Of course it is nice to ride a good-looking horse; but in the mountains most emphatically "handsome is what handsome does." The horses I now own are fine animals and fine mountain ponies; but some of the best I have ever ridden, a horseman would not look at twice. On a time, being under the absolute necessity of getting a pack quickly, I purchased a bay that I promptly named Methuselah. He was some sixteen years old, badly stove forward by hard riding, and not much of a horse anyway. For three months he carried a pack. Then one day I threw a saddle on him to go a short distance on some little errand. Methuselah, overjoyed, did his best. The old horse was one of the best mountain saddlers in the outfit. He climbed surely and well; he used his head in negotiating bad places; would stay where he was put. The fact that he was not sound was utterly unimportant, for not once in a week was he required to go faster than a walk.

On the other hand I once owned a Bill-horse, mountain-bred and raised. He was a beautiful beast, proud, high-stepping—one you would be glad to be seen on. He would have been worth considerable money, and would have afforded much solid satisfaction if I had wanted him for cow work, or pleasure riding in the lower country. But it was absolutely impossible to catch him, even hobbled, without a corral. One day I saw him leap from a stand and with hobbles over a fence and feed trough. So I traded him for another, not near so much of a horse, as a horse, but worth two dozen Bill-horses.

Gun Shyness

What One "Sam Fat" Did

One other thing you must notice, and that is whether or not the beast is gun shy. A great many stampede wildly at the report of firearms. I once owned a pack horse named Sam Fat, on which for some time I congratulated myself. He was a heavy animal, and could carry a tremendous load; and yet he was sure-footed and handled himself well on rough country. He was gentle and friendly. He took excellent care of his pack, and he followed perfectly. No one needed to ride behind him to keep Sam Fat coming. I used to turn him loose when I started, and pay no more attention to him until I stopped. No matter how rich the feed through which we passed, Sam Fat was always on hand when the halt was called. And, very important point, he was a good rustler—he kept fat and sleek on poor food where other horses gaunted. Altogether Sam Fat was a find. Then one day one of the party shot off a harmless little twenty-two caliber popgun. Sam Fat went crazy. He squatted flat, uttered a terrified squeal, and departed through the woods, banging his pack against trees and hanging limbs. We chased him a mile, and finally brought him back, but all the rest of the day he was panicky. I tried to get him accustomed to shooting by tying him near our target practice, but it was no use. Finally, though reluctantly, I sold him.

So when the natives bring in their horses for your selection blind your eyes to the question of looks and points until you have divided the offering into two parts—those that are sure-footed, courageous, gentle, tractable, easy to catch, good grub rustlers, and if pack horses, those that will follow and will take care of their packs, and those that lack one or more of these qualifications. Discard the second group. Then if the first group contains nothing but blemished or homely horses, make the best of it, perfectly sure that the others might as well not exist.

Qualifications

In general, a horse just from pasture should have a big belly. A small-bellied horse will prove to be a poor feeder, and will probably weaken down on a long hike. The best horse stands from fourteen hands to fourteen two, and is chunkily built. There are exceptions, both ways, to this rule. A pack horse is better with low withers on account of the possibility of sore backs. Avoid a horse whose ears hang sidewise from his head; he is apt to be stubborn. As for the rest, horse sense is the same everywhere.

What a Horse Should Carry

Sore Backs

A pack horse can carry two hundred pounds—not more. Of course more can be piled on him, and he will stand up under it, but on a long trip he will deteriorate. Greater weights are carried only in text books, in camp-fire lies, and where a regular pack route permits of grain feeding. A good animal, with care, will take two hundred successfully enough, but I personally always pack much lighter. Feed costs nothing, so it is every bit as cheap to take three horses as two. The only expense is the slight bother of packing an extra animal. In return you can travel farther and more steadily, the chances of sore backs are minimized, your animals keep fat and strong, and in case one meets with an accident, you can still save all your effects on the other. For the last three years I have made it a practice to pack only about a hundred to a hundred and twenty-five pounds when off for a very long trip. My animals have always come out fat and hearty, sometimes in marked contrast to those of my companions, and I have not had a single case of sore back.

The latter are best treated by Bickmore's Gall Cure. Its use does not interfere in the least with packing; and I have never seen a case it did not cure inside ten days or two weeks if applied at the beginning of the trouble.

How Far a Horse Should Travel

In the mountains and on grass-feed twenty miles a day is big travel. If you push more than that you are living beyond your income. It is much better, if you are moving every day, to confine yourself to jaunts of from twelve to fifteen miles on an average. Then if necessity arises, you have something to fall back on, and are able to make a forced march.

Mountain Travel

The distance may seem very short to you if you have never traveled in the mountains; but as a matter of fact you will probably find it quite sufficient, both in length of time and in variety of scenery. To cover it you will travel steadily for from six to eight hours; and in the diversity of country will be interested every step of the way. Indeed so varied will be the details that it will probably be difficult to believe you have made so small a mileage, until you stop to reflect that, climbing and resting, no horse can go faster than two or two and one-half miles an hour.

Desert Travel

On the desert or the plains the length of your journey must depend entirely on the sort of feed you can get. Thirty miles a day for a long period is all a fed-horse can do, while twenty is plenty enough for an animal depending on his own foraging. Longer rides are not to be considered in the course of regular travel. I once did one hundred and eighty miles in two days—and then took a rest.

Time to Travel

In the mountains you must keep in mind that a horse must both eat and rest; and that he will not graze when frost is on the meadows. Many otherwise skillful mountaineers ride until nearly dark, and are up and off soon after daylight. They wonder why their horses lose flesh and strength. The truth is the poor beasts must compress their twenty-four hours of sustenance into the short noon stop, and the shorter evening before the frost falls. It is often much wiser to get a very early start, to travel until the middle of the afternoon, and then to go into camp. Whatever inconvenience and discomfort you may suffer is more than made up for by the opportunities to hunt, fish, or cook afforded by the early stop; and the time you imagine you lose is regained in the long run by the regularity of your days' journeys.

Desert Journeying

On the desert or the plains where it is hot, to the contrary, you will have better luck by traveling early and late. Desert journeying is uncomfortable anyway, but has its compensations. We ordinarily get under way by three in the morning; keep going until nine; start about six again—after supper—and travel until nine of the evening. Thus we take advantage of whatever coolness is possible, and see the rising and the falling of the day, which is the most wonderful and beautiful of the desert's gifts.

Climbing

Going up steep hills in high altitudes you must breathe your horse every fifty feet or so. It need not be a long rest. Merely rein him in for eight or ten seconds. Do the same thing *always* before entering the negotiation of a bad place in the trail. Do this, no matter how fresh and eager your animal may seem. Often it spells the difference between a stumble and a good clean climb. An experienced pack horse will take these rests on his own initiative, stopping and also starting again with the regularity of clockwork.

It does not hurt a horse to sweat, but if ever he begins to drip heavily, and to tremble in the legs, it is getting time to hunt the shade for a rest. I realize that such minor points as these may be perfectly well known to every one likely to read this book, and yet I have seen so many cases of ignorance of them on the trail that I risk their inclusion here.

Unsaddling

Every hour or so loosen the cinches of your saddle horse and raise the saddle and blankets an inch or so to permit a current of air to pass through. Steaming makes the back tender. When you unsaddle him or the pack animals, if they are very hot, leave the blankets across them for a few moments. A hot sun shining on a sweaty back causes small pimples, which may develop into sores. It is better to bathe with cold water the backs of green horses; but such a trouble is not necessary after they are hardened.

To Pick Up a Horse's Feet

Two more things I will mention, though strictly speaking, they do not fall in the province of equipment. When you pick up a horse's hind foot, face to the rear, put the hand nearest the horse firmly against his flank, and use the other to raise the hoof. Then if he tries to kick, you can hold him off sufficiently to get out of the way. Indeed the very force of his movement toward you will thrust against the hand on his flank and tend to throw you to one side.

To Mount a Bad Horse

If you are called upon to mount a bad horse, seize the check piece of his bridle in your left hand and twist his head sharply toward you. At the same time grasp the pommel in your right hand, thrust your foot in the stirrup and swing aboard. Never get on any western horse as an easterner mounts—left hand on pommel and right hand on cantle. If a horse plunges forward to buck while you are in this position, you will inevitably land back of the saddle. Then he has a fine leverage to throw you about forty feet. A bad pack horse you can handle by blindfolding. Anchor things for a storm, take off the bandage, and stand one side.

CHAPTER XII
CANOES

I suppose I have paddled about every sort of craft in use, and have found good qualities in all. Now that I am called upon to pick out one of them and label it as the best, even for a specific purpose, I must confess myself puzzled as to a choice. Perhaps the best way would be to describe the different sorts of canoe in common use, detail their advantages, tell what I consider the best of each kind, and leave the choice to your own taste or the circumstances in which you may find yourself.

Kinds of Canoes

Practicable canoes are made of birch bark stretched over light frames; of cedar; of basswood; of canvas, and of canvas cover over stiff frames.

The Birch Bark

Advantages and Disadvantages

The birch bark canoe has several unassailable advantages. It is light; it carries a greater weight in proportion to its length than any other; it is very easily mended. On the other hand it is not nearly so fast as a wooden canoe of sweeter lines; does not bear transportation so well; is more easily punctured; and does not handle so readily in a heavy wind. These advantages and disadvantages, as you can see, balance against one another. If it tends to veer in a heavy wind more than the wooden canoe, it is lighter on portage. If more fragile, it is very easily mended. If it is not quite so fast, it carries more duffle. Altogether, it is a very satisfactory all-around craft in which I have paddled many hundreds of miles, and with which I have never been seriously dissatisfied. If I were to repeat some long explorations in the absolute wilds of Canada I should choose a birch canoe, if only for the reason that no matter how badly I might smash it, the materials are always at hand for repairs. A strip of bark from the nearest birch tree; a wad of gum from the next spruce; some spruce roots; a little lard and a knife will mend a canoe stove in utterly.

Getting ready for another day of it

Selection of a Birch Bark

In selecting a birch bark canoe the most important thing to look after is to see that the bottom is all one piece without projecting knots or mended cracks. Many canoes have bottoms made of two pieces. These when grounded almost invariably spring a leak at the seam, for the simple reason that it takes very little to scrape off the slightly projecting gum. On the other hand, a bottom of one good piece of bark will stand an extraordinary amount of raking and bumping without being any the worse. If in addition you can get hold of one made of the winter cut of bark, the outside shell will be as good as possible. Try to purchase a new canoe. Should this be impossible, look well to the *watap*, or roots, used in the sewing, that they are not frayed or burst. The frames should lie so close together as fairly to touch. Such a canoe, "two fathoms," will carry two men and four hundred pounds besides. It will weigh about fifty to seventy pounds, and should cost new from six to eight dollars.

Cedar and Basswood

A wooden canoe, of some sort, is perhaps better for all smooth and open-water sailing, and all short trips nearer home. It will stand a great deal of jamming about, but is very difficult to mend if ever you do punch a hole in it. You will need to buy a longer craft than when getting a birch. The latter will run from twelve to fourteen feet. A wood canoe of that length would float gunwhale awash at half you would wish to carry. Seventeen or eighteen feet is small enough for two men, although I have cruised in smaller. Cedar is the lighter material—and the more expensive—but splits too readily. Basswood is heavier, but is cheaper and tougher.

The Folding Canvas

The folding canvas boat is an abomination. It is useful only as a craft from which to fish in an inaccessible spot. Sooner or later it sags and gives, and so becomes logy.

Canvas Covered

A canoe is made, however, and much used by the Hudson's Bay Company, exactly on the frame of a birch bark, but covered with tightly stretched and painted canvas. It is a first-rate craft, combining an approach to the lightness of the birch bark with the sweeter lines of the wooden canoe. All ordinary small tears in its bottom are easily patched by the gum method. Its only inferiority to the birch rests in the facts that it is more easily torn; that a major accident, such as the smashing of an entire bow, cannot be as readily mended; and that it will not carry quite so great a weight. All in all, however, it is a good and serviceable canoe.

Portaging

In portaging, I have always had pretty good luck with the primitive Indian fashion—the two paddles lengthwise across the thwarts and resting on the shoulders, with perhaps a sweater or other padding to relieve the pressure. It is possible, however, to buy cushions which just fit, and on which you can kneel while paddling, and also a regular harness to distribute the weight. I should think they might be very good, and would certainly be no trouble to carry. Only that makes one more thing to look after, and the job can perfectly well be done without.

Paddles

The Indian paddle is a very long and very narrow blade, just as long as the height of its wielder. For use in swift and somewhat shallow water, where often the paddle must be thrust violently against the bottom or a rock, this form is undoubtedly the best. In more open, or smoother water, however, the broader and shorter blade is better, though even in the latter case it is well to select one of medium length. Otherwise you will find yourself, in a heavy sea, sometimes reaching rather frantically down toward the water. Whatever its length, attach it to the thwart nearest you by a light strong line. Then if you should go overboard you will retain control of your craft. I once swam over a mile before I was able to overtake a light canoe carried forward by a lively wind.

Setting Poles

On any trip wherein you may have to work your way back against the current, you must carry an iron "shoe" to fit on a setting pole. Any blacksmith can make you one. Have it constructed with nail holes. Then when you want a setting pole, you can cut one in the woods, and nail to it your iron shoe.

Knapsacks

The harness for packs is varied enough, but the principle remains simple. A light pack will hang well enough from the shoulders, but when any weight is to be negotiated you must call into play the powerful muscles lying along the neck. Therefore, in general, an ordinary knapsack will answer very well for packs up to say thirty pounds. Get the straps broad and soft; see that they are both sewed and riveted.

Tumplines

How to Carry Packs

When, however, your pack mounts to above thirty pounds you will need some sort of strap to pass across the top of your head. This is known as a tumpline, and consists of a band of leather to cross the head, and two long thongs to secure the pack. The blanket or similar cloth is spread, the thongs laid lengthwise about a foot from either edge, and the blanket folded inward and across the thongs. The things to be carried are laid on the end of the blanket toward the head piece. The other end of the blanket, from the folds of which the ends of the thongs are protruding, is then laid up over the pile. The ends of the thongs are then pulled tight, tied together, and passed around the middle of the pack. To carry this outfit with any degree of comfort, be sure to get it low, fairly in the small of the back or even just above the hips. A compact and heavy article, such as a sack of flour, is a much simpler matter. The thongs are tied together at a suitable distance. One side of the loop thus formed goes around your head, and the other around the sack of flour.

It will not slip.

Tumplines.

Pack Harnesses

By far the best and most comfortable pack outfit I have used is a combination of the shoulder and the head methods. It consists of shoulder harness like that used on knapsacks, with two long straps and buckles to pass around and secure any load. A tumpline is attached to the top of the knapsack straps. I have carried in this contrivance over a hundred pounds without discomfort. Suitable adjustment of the headstrap will permit you to relieve alternately your neck and shoulders. Heavy or rather compact articles can be included in the straps, while the bulkier affairs will rest very well on top of the pack. It is made by Abercrombie & Fitch, and costs two dollars and seventy-five cents.

INDEX

A

B

I

J

K

L

M

O

P

Q

R

S

T

Y

Lector House believes that a society develops through a two-fold approach of continuous learning and adaptation, which is derived from the study of classic literary works spread across the historic timeline of literature records. Therefore, we aim at reviving, repairing and redeveloping all those inaccessible or damaged but historically as well as culturally important literature across subjects so that the future generations may have an opportunity to study and learn from past works to embark upon a journey of creating a better future.

This book is a result of an effort made by Lector House towards making a contribution to the preservation and repair of original ancient works which might hold historical significance to the approach of continuous learning across subjects.

HAPPY READING & LEARNING!

LECTOR HOUSE

LECTOR HOUSE LLP

E-MAIL: info@lectorhouse.com

9 789356 145887

9 789356 145887

Printed by Libri Plureos GmbH in Hamburg,
Germany